We wish to thank Ron Adair (www.ronadair.com) for supplying the art work for the book cover. Ron's use and direction of light, both on the ground and the sky has a redemptive motif. The actual cross is off to the left, out of view, with its shadow visible. The blue sky depicts righteousness—emanating from the cross—and the clouds indicate sin that is progressively being pushed aside. The area and shape of blue is decisive and sharp—not blurry or blended with the clouds—as it penetrates the turbulence. The light is dynamic and moving toward and displacing the darkness. "Then spake Jesus again unto them, saying, I am the light of the world: he that followeth me shall not walk in darkness, but shall have the light of life." John 8:12

DEFINITE ATONEMENT

GARY D. LONG

5317 Wye Creek Drive, Frederick, MD 21703-6938

phone: 301-473-8781 or 800-376-4146   fax: 240-206-0373
email: info@newcovenantmedia.com
Website: www.newcovenantmedia.com

DEFINITE ATONEMENT

Second Edition © 1977 by Gary D. Long
Third Edition © 2006 by Gary D. Long

ISBN-13: 978-1-9289765-17-6
ISBN-10: 1-928965-17-2

Requests for information should be addressed to:
New Covenant Media
5317 Wye Creek Drive
Frederick, MD 21703-6938

Scripture quotations are taken from the King James Version of the Holy Bible.

To the Triune Jehovah
to whom salvation belongs,
I dedicate this book
(Jonah 2:9)

TABLE OF CONTENTS

FOREWORD

It is a distinct pleasure for me to write a foreword to the second edition of Gary Long's very helpful and useful book, *Definite Atonement,* first published in 1976.

My long friendship with Dr. Long goes back to the years in which he was a student and I a professor at Dallas Theological Seminary in Dallas, Texas. In those days we had many conversations and times together, not only in the classes in New Testament exegesis of the Greek text on New Testament books, but also outside the classroom. I look back upon those years as a time of further spiritual and theological growth for me.

My own theological position at the time was what might be called Amyraldian, although not strictly true to historical Amyraldism, or hypothetical universalism. I frequently used the term, "four point Calvinist," to express my view, although I did not use the term, as so many fundamentally Arminian evangelicals do today, as a kind of code term meaning, "I am against limited atonement." I really did believe in the bondage of the will and rejected the capital Arminian doctrine of free will, embraced by so many evangelicals calling themselves "Calvinists," or "mild Calvinists."

The personal debt that I owe to Dr. Long consists in the fact that, through our talks together and the further study of the question of particular redemption in the Scriptures under the guidance of the Holy Spirit, which they fostered, I was brought to an understanding and acceptance of consistent soteriological Calvinism. Arising out of that, of course, came a deeper appreciation for and a deeper knowledge of the doctrine of sovereign grace, which I can never associate with anything other than the great doctrines of human inability, unconditional election, definite atonement, efficacious grace, and the perseverance of the saints.

I am, therefore, very indebted to Dr. Long and to the insights that he shared with me concerning the biblical doctrine of grace.

He was a fine student in his work at the seminary, and I believe that this is evidenced in his book, which was originally a master's thesis presented to the seminary as part of the requirements for the degree of Th.M.

While Dr. Long has been a careful student of the original text of the New Testament, as well as being especially interested in the discipline of biblical theology, it is as a theological thinker that one will come to admire the author from this fine book. The work is grounded in sound exegesis of the text, something singularly missing in much of contemporary theological writing. And it is well informed on the issues that touch the question of the particularism of the atoning work of Christ.

The method of treatment of the issue that Dr. Long has followed is both theological and exegetical. The first part of the work is theological, and the author argues persuasively and quite thoroughly for the accomplishment of a definite atonement by our Lord in His death upon Calvary's cross. As an Appendix he has treated in exegetical detail the leading texts offered by Arminians in objection to the author's position. The texts dealt with are 2 Peter 2:1, 1 John 2:2 and 2 Corinthians 5:19. Thus, there is both theology and exegesis in the defense.

It is often said by beleaguered Arminians that Calvinism is logical and consistent, but that the texts favor their view. Of course, one might simply reply, "Shall we prefer that which is illogical and inconsistent to logical consistency?" Would it not be better to begin with logical consistency and examine in a bit more depth our exegesis? The latter course is surely a more intelligent approach, and Dr. Long's work is a fine place at which to begin. His handling of the texts mentioned above should help anyone to see that there are consistent and appealing interpretations that are harmonious with the doctrine of particular redemption. In fact, Dr. Long generally points out that there are several possibilities of interpretation that are harmonious with the Calvinistic viewpoint on these debated texts, and he does not demand that we follow his views puppet-like.

Of course, as Dr. Long points out also, all of the texts that teach the doctrine of penal substitution are texts that support fully the Calvinistic viewpoint. That is one of the reasons that Arminians have generally favored a governmental view of the atonement. If we grant that the atonement is a substitutionary one, then all of the texts that teach substitution affirm the Calvinistic view. Since the New Testament is filled with texts teaching penal substitution, from our Lord through the apostles, it can no longer be claimed by any intelligent student of the question that, while logic favors Calvinism, the texts do not. The alternative is the denial of substitution and the admission that, since evangelicals cannot accept universal salvation, that some will pay for their sins twice, one in Christ's death and then in theirs.

Dr. Long has much more to say on the point, such as, "if Christ has truly borne the sins of all men in penal substitution, there is nothing left for divine justice to punish" [p. 37]. Any reader will profit from the things the author has to say on the subject in Chapter III.

Over one hundred years ago Patrick Hues Mell, a prominent Southern Baptist minister and defender of the doctrine of sovereign grace in the nineteenth century, lamented the tendencies in his day to soft pedal the apostolic doctrine of grace. "I have been pained to notice, for some years past, on the part of some of our ministers, in some localities in the South," Mell wrote, "a disposition to waive the doctrines of Grace in their public ministrations. While some have been entirely silent about them and have even preached, though not ostensibly, doctrines not consistent with them, others have given them only a cold and half-hearted assent, and some few have openly derided and denounced them" (P. H. Mell, *Predestination and the Saints' Perseverance, Stated and Defended* [Charleston: Southern

Baptist Publication Society, 1851]). It is just this failure in our day to which Dr. Long's book is dedicated and ably suited to correct.

There are so many useful and helpful discussions of important aspects of the doctrine of God's grace in this book that I can only say, "Read it! Ponder it! And embrace the truth! It will be mind-clearing, heart-warming, and spiritually nourishing."

Perhaps I may be allowed to make one final comment. To my mind the concept of the universal and spiritually egalitarian love of God lies at the base of a great deal of the spiritual failure of our day. In fact, it is a doctrine that is eminently calculated to give comfort to the apathetic and indifferent among us, who seem to be dwelling in a spiritual coma.

There is, of course, a twofold love of God, that for the non-elect and that for the elect. While great benefits accrue to the non-elect from Christ's atoning work, including the blessings of common grace and coming to high expression in the entreaties, the overtures, and the imperatives of gospel preaching, there is nevertheless a radical difference between the benefits of divine love as they pertain to the non-elect and the elect. The difference lies in the distinguishing love that ensures for the elect that they will be partakers of the atonement. It corresponds to the distinguishing nature of divine election.

I heartily recommend Dr. Long's discussion of God's eternal love, immutable and distinguishing. It is surely a needed warning to the complacent and an antidote to evangelicalism's current superficiality in the preaching of divine grace.

I am indeed thankful to God that a new edition of *Definite Atonement* is on the way, and I look forward to seeing it published with great anticipation.

S. Lewis Johnson, Jr.
August 1977

2005 PREFACE

Definite Atonement has been out of print for some time. This new edition makes only minor changes to the 1977 edition and clarifies in Chapter 2 the relationship of God's eternal purpose and its fulfillment in the "blood of the everlasting covenant," that is, in Christ, the mediator of the New Covenant.

The reader will find that I have made little change to the annotated selected bibliography at the end of this book. The reason is that those works still stand as good, representative bibliographical references. Some of the works listed have been reprinted and may be found by a web search—an easy task in the modern tech world. I will mention only one work not contained in the bibliography—there could have been more—which provides an excellent and articulate pamphlet entitled, *Limited Atonement*. It is written by my good and long time friend of 35 years, John G. Reisinger—a true warrior for the gospel of Christ. It was published in 2002 by the publisher of this new edition of *Definite Atonement*.

I am indebted for the republishing of this edition to the encouragement of many of my friends and readers of the previous edition of *Definite Atonement*. I want to again acknowledge one of my most influential mentors, Dr. S. Lewis Johnson, Jr., who departed this life in January 2004 to be present with our Lord. His faithful obedience to the contextual teaching of the Word of God and its interpretative principles has greatly influenced me in my understanding of the sacred Scriptures. I also want to thank Jacob Moseley of New Covenant Media who has helped me with the *mechanics* of getting this book republished. Finally, I must thank by wife, Barbara, again for encouraging me in my life's ministry including this edition of *Definite Atonement*. [As an addendum to my family, I should mention that I have another daughter, Gloriann, who was not born at the time of the earlier edition when her older sister and two brothers were mentioned.

All four of our children are now married and belong to Christ. Barbara and I are currently blessed with nine grandchildren.]

May this new edition of *Definite Atonement* prove to be of much help to many who have believed and many who will believe through grace.

Gary D. Long
September 19, 2005

1977 PREFACE

The primary purpose of this book is to set forth, in readable form, a positive polemic for the doctrine of definite atonement from the standpoint of the design and outworkings of each member of the triune Godhead in saving lost sinners. If I were asked: "What is the strongest support for definite atonement?" I would unhesitatingly answer, "The eternality and immutability of God's special distinguishing love" based upon Romans 8:32 and John 3:16, in context. (An annotated doctrinal sermon outline on definite atonement is contained at Appendix IV.)

Because of the positive design of Chapters I-V, most of the technical and apologetic remarks are placed in footnotes or in appendixes. Specifically, Appendixes I-III are expressly written to answer what universal redemptionists assert to be the strongest biblical defense for indefinite atonement—a defense based upon three doctrinal terms in three verses of Scripture: redemption (II Pet. 2:1); propitiation (I John 2:2); and reconciliation (II Cor. 5:19). A detailed discussion of the major theological interpretations of these three key verses is contained in Appendixes I-III, respectively. A summary rather than a thorough discussion of the theological interpretations of each of these verses was considered. However, it is my belief that the detailed approach will be preferred by the reader who is truly interested in studying the extent of the atonement. It is concluded that II Peter 2:1, I John 2:2, and II Corinthians 5:19 provide no theological bases for supporting an indefinite atonement, especially when they are fairly examined by consistent principles of biblical interpretation. Other passages that are set forth as biblical proof for unlimited atonement (e.g., I Tim. 2:4, 6; 4:10; Titus 2:11; II Pet. 3:9) are not specifically addressed in this work for the simple reason that, if redemption, propitiation, and reconciliation are designed for and applied only to the elect, the atonement of Christ cannot be indefinite or unlimited in design for all mankind without exception. (A summary chart of four major problem verses on the extent of the atonement concerning the will of God is contained at Appendix V.)

In brief, I see no purpose, benefit, or comfort in an atonement that does not redeem, a propitiation that does not propitiate, a reconciliation that does not reconcile; neither do I have any faith in a hypothetical salvation for hypothetical believers. Rather, I have faith in an atonement which infallibly secures the salvation of each and every one for whom it was designed, namely, "the children of God that were scattered abroad" (John 11:52), which is such a multitude of sinners declared righteous that no one can number them.

My desire for those who read this book is that they read and study it through in its entirety. I do not ask or expect that all Calvinists will agree with it, but I do ask both the modified Calvinists and evangelical Arminians to understand it objectively and to quote from it contextually. It is also my earnest desire that the reader should understand that my opposition to the doctrine of indefinite atonement is a doctrinal issue and not a personal attack upon those who espouse indefinite atonement. Every born again believer should be ready to have his theological views judged by Scripture without taking personal affront. Therefore, a distinction must be made between the errors propounded by Christians and the Christians themselves. All that are within the circle of Christ's love must be within the circle of the Christian's love. To contend for doctrine in a manner which ignores this truth is a rending of the unity of the true Church, which is Christ's body, the elect of God.

Many friends have been of assistance and encouragement in the preparation of this work. My wife, Barbara, has been a most constructive critic and faithful helpmeet throughout all the time of study, research and preparation. In the mystery of God's providence, it was her faithfulness and prayers and the godly influence of my younger brother, Jackie, and Colonel Ira A. Palm (both now deceased and present with the Lord), which the triune

God used as means to save me. To each of them, in the Lord, I am and shall be eternally grateful. I thank Loraine Boettner and S. Lewis Johnson, Jr., for their special encouragement and help, first, by their lives, and, second, by their constructive remarks and critical review of the manuscript. Dr. Johnson was of particular help to me during my seminary years (1965-72) at Dallas Theological Seminary, where I first wrote this work in with a detailed exegetical analysis of II Peter 2:1 and a lengthy bibliography, but without Appendixes II-V.

Finally, I want to express by heartfelt gratitude for my three children, Gina, Grant, and Gary David, who were most patient and understanding during the preparation of this work; for the love of my parents, Mr. and Mrs. Orville Long of Bethany, Missouri; for Stanley Owen, a pastor in Columbia, Missouri, who first introduced me to the doctrines of grace; and for those during 1972-1975 who in Grace Reformed Fellowship in Copperas Cove, Texas "believed through grace" and are a genuine blessing to me in the pastoral ministry.

Gary D. Long
August 15, 1977

CHAPTER I

INTRODUCTION

Background

Through the teachings of Moyse Amyraut (1596-1664), the theological father of Calvinistic or hypothetical universalism (four point Calvinism), an attempt was made to smooth the "harshness" of Calvinism with the design of "arousing less repulsion in Roman Catholics and in Arminians, and of providing a more suitable basis of union with the Lutherans."[1] But A. A. Hodge, citing an article in the original Herzog's Encyclopaedia, wrote that Amyraut, toward the close of his life, came to see that there was nothing real in all his new distinctions to support his attempt to smooth this harshness by teaching a Calvinistic universalism.[2] A summarization of the attempt to harmonize Arminianism and Calvinism on this issue was aptly stated by Hodge over one hundred years ago when he wrote:

> Unquestionably there is no compromise between Arminianism and Calvinism. Those who attempt to stand between must content themselves with treading the air while they receive the fire of both sides. We do not object to Calvinistic Universalism ... because of any danger with which—when considered as a final position—it threatens orthodoxy. We distrust it rather because it is not a final position, but is the first step in the easy descent of error.[3]

In light of the above, it should be apparent that a scriptural view of the design or extent of the atonement, which is in harmony with the whole of Scripture, is essential if one is to teach consistently and preach the "so great salvation" planned,

---

[1] Roger Nicole, Thesis Abstract on "Moyse Amyraut (1596-1664) and the Controversy on Universal Grace: First Phase (1634-1637)" (unpublished Ph.D. dissertation, Department of Church History, Harvard University, 1966).

[2] Archibald Alexander Hodge, *The Atonement* (reprint of 1867 ed.; Cherry Hill, NJ: Mack Publishing Co., n.d.), 238.

[3] *Ibid.*

accomplished and applied by the triune God. Inconsistency in this area, especially since Amyraut's day, has historically led to more serious theological and practical error and deluded many who are otherwise evangelical in their faith into believing and teaching that the merits of the atoning work of Christ are so infinite that every member of Adam's race is redeemed and can be saved if he or she only chooses to will it.

Terminology

In studying the design of the atonement, one of the first questions which must be answered is "whether the Scripture teaches that the Father in sending the Son and the Son in offering Himself did intend to provide salvation for all men and every man or whether they [the triune God] intended to secure the salvation of all those and those only who will in fact be redeemed."[4]

Thus the design or the extent of the atonement involves the intent; that is, whom did the triune God intend to save through the redemptive work of Christ? Some refer to this doctrine as the doctrine of "limited atonement"—the term denoted by the third letter in the mnemonic "TULIP": Total depravity, Unconditional election, Limited atonement, Irresistible grace, and I perseverance of the saints. These five doctrines became known as the "five points of Calvinism." They were the Calvinists' answer at the Synod of Dort in 1618 to the five points of Arminianism previously formulated in Holland in 1610.[5] Regrettably, the term "limited atonement" has often been misunderstood to mean that Christ's atonement was limited in its efficacy rather than its

---

[4]Roger Nicole, "The Case for Definite Atonement," *Bulletin of the Evangelical Theological Society* X, *no.* 4 (1967): 200.

[5]Cf. J. 1. Packer, "Introductory Essay" to John Owen's *The Death of Death in the Death of Christ* (added to a reprint from Vol. X of Owen's Works published in 1852 by Johnstone and Hunter, Edinburgh, ed. William H. Goold; London: Banner of Truth Trust, 1959), 3-6.

intended design. That this should not be the case was well stated by Spurgeon when he remarked:

We are often told that we limit the atonement of Christ, because we say that Christ has not made a satisfaction for all men, or all men would be saved. Now, our reply to this is, that, on the other hand, our opponents limit it, we do not. The Arminians say, Christ died for all men. Ask them what they mean by it. Did Christ die so as to secure the salvation of all men? They say, "No, certainly not." We ask them the next question—Did Christ die so as to secure the salvation of any man in particular? They answer "No." They are obliged to admit this, if they are consistent. They say "No; Christ has died that any man may be saved if'—and then follow certain conditions of salvation. We say, then, we will just go back to the old statement—Christ did not die so as beyond a doubt to secure the salvation of anybody, did he? You must say "No"; you are obliged to say so, for you believe that even after a man has been pardoned, he may yet fall from grace, and perish. Now, who is it that limits the death of Christ? Why, you. You say that Christ did not die so as to infallibly secure the salvation of anybody. We beg your pardon, when you say we limit Christ's death; we say, "No, my dear sir, it is you that do it." We say Christ so died that he infallibly secured the salvation of a multitude that no man can number, who through Christ's death not only may be saved, but are saved, must be saved, and cannot by any possibility run the hazard of being anything but saved. You are welcome to your atonement; you may keep it. We will never renounce ours for the sake of it.[6]

Due to the frequent misunderstanding of the term "limited atonement," I prefer the terms "definite atonement" and "particular redemption." Therefore, these latter two terms will be used interchangeably in this work to refer to the doctrine as stated above.

---

[6]Charles Haddon Spurgeon, "Particular Redemption," Sermon 181 in the *New Park Street Pulpit* (reprint of the 1st ed. published by Alabaster, Passmore and Sons in 1859; Grand Rapids: Zondervan Publishing House, 1964), 4:135.

The Need

The work of the triune God in salvation is little understood, even by professing Christians. In many evangelical churches where the Lord Jesus is still formally acknowledged to be the only Saviour, the current teaching of the day, in reference to the design of the atonement, is that Christ has made it possible for all men to be saved. He did this by dying a provisional, substitutionary death for the sin of the world. However, the individual must, by his own free will,[7] decide for himself whether or not he shall be saved before Christ's atonement becomes an actual substitution for his sins. Those who are more Arminian than Calvinistic in their theology assert that the atoning work of Christ did not and does not secure the salvation of anyone in particular. As a result of this teaching, particularly in America during the last two centuries, man's total spiritual depravity is often denied in practice by both evangelical Arminians and modified Calvinists, and the idea now widely prevails that Christ is offered to man's acceptance and that he must "accept Christ as his personal Saviour," "give his heart to Jesus," "open up his heart and let Jesus come in" in order for the blood of the cross to avail for him as a lost sinner. But, if this is not done, the fact that Christ died for his sins remains true and the rejection of Christ's atonement now becomes the sole basis for his condemnation.[8] Accordingly, out of theological necessity, it follows from those who teach this view (especially the four point Calvinists) that the substitutionary aspect of Christ's death, that is, for the guilt and penalty of sin, is applied only to the elect but not to the non-elect

---

[7] Cf. a discussion on the ambiguity of the term "will" in my "Doctrine of Original Sin in New England Theology: From Jonathan Edwards to Edwards Amasa Park" (unpublished Th. D. dissertation, Dallas Theological Seminary, 1972), 14-16.

[8] Robert P. Lightner, *The Death Christ Died–A Case for Unlimited Atonement* (Des Plaines, Illinois: Regular Baptist Press, 1967), 43, 46-47, 52, 56, 99, 101, 145.

because of their persistence in unbelief. However, they say Christ was a substitute for the non-elect only in a governmental or legal sense; that is, He removed the legal obstacles standing in the way of their salvation, and, on account of this legal substitution, a warrant or basis upon which the free offer of the gospel rests[9] has been provided and thereby a just basis exists for condemning the non-elect because of their rejection of Him as the only way of salvation.

It is strongly implied in practice, but usually denied theologically, by many who believe in universal redemption, even by modified Calvinists, that one's believing in Christ is a contributory cause rather than an effect of regeneration. But the theological denial by modified Calvinists that saving faith is a cooperative work of man in salvation is frequently inconsistent with their preaching. One only has to listen to or read the close of their sermons to observe this fact. Such inconsistent preaching by the modified Calvinist and the typical preaching by the evangelical Arminian reduces to making saving faith a cooperative effort between God and man; that is, if man is willing to believe, God will then enable him to do so. This is why

---

[9]Out of a sincere desire to establish a warrant of faith to freely offer the gospel to all mankind without exception, many four point Calvinists (even some five point Calvinists) theologically sound on the nature of the atonement, have held to this twofold aspect of substitution in various form and degree of emphasis. Examples of modified Calvinist representatives are Ralph Wardlaw, an early nineteenth century theologian from Scotland, and, on the contemporary scene, Norman F. Douty, who recently published a work supporting unlimited or indefinite atonement entitled: *"The Death of Christ."* The Marrow men of the Scottish Secession Church in the early eighteenth century are examples of five point Calvinist representatives, and there are indications that some contemporary five point Calvinists are wavering in this area. Historically, through the use of dubious language, this twofold aspect of the atonement has led to more serious departures from the truth. It occurred in the history of New England theology which, after Jonathan Edwards (d. 1758), drifted almost exclusively to a governmental view of the atonement. Cf. my dissertation on the "Doctrine of Original Sin in New England Theology," 206.

evangelical Arminians believing in a universal redemption deny that saving faith is wholly a gift from God. But is this not saying that, ultimately, the finished work of Christ is left contingent on the will of man rather than the will of God? Is this not clearly in contradiction with John 1:13 and James 1:18? Certainly it is. As a result, saving faith is viewed (if not by the preacher, then by the hearer) as a conditional work of man rather than a gift of sovereign grace. Hence, man is exalted, God is belittled, and the grace of God is cheapened. Therefore, I believe that there is a genuine need for a work on definite atonement written from a positive polemical approach.

Purpose

In view of the need, the purpose of this work is to set forth, in a positive manner, some of the major theological proofs for the doctrine of definite atonement.

It is my firm conviction that the five points of Calvinism perfectly harmonize with the biblical truth that salvation belongs to the triune Jehovah. Therefore, not one of the so-called "five points" can be consistently rejected without scripturally or logically rejecting all of them. In some ways it is unfortunate that the term "Calvinism" is applied to these doctrines. But it is used, as Spurgeon declared a century ago, because:

> I have my own private opinion that there is no such thing as preaching Christ and Him crucified, unless we preach what nowadays is called Calvinism. It is a nickname to call it Calvinism; Calvinism is the gospel, and nothing else. I do not believe we can preach the gospel, if we do not preach justification by faith without works; nor unless we preach the sovereignty of God in His dispensation of grace; nor unless we exalt the electing unchangeable eternal, immutable, conquering love of Jehovah; nor do I think we can preach the gospel, unless we base it upon the special and

particular redemption of His elect and chosen people which Christ wrought out upon the cross.[10]

It is the purpose of this work to set forth theological proof for the third of the "five points of Calvinism"—the doctrine of definite atonement—in order to help recover the old, authentic, biblical gospel and to help bring evangelical teaching, preaching and practice back into line with it.

---

[10]Charles Haddon Spurgeon, *The Early Years* (rev. ed.; London: The Banner of Truth Trust, 1962), 168.

Some Questions to Consider Concerning the Doctrine of Salvation

1. Will or can anyone of himself seek after God (Rom. 3:10-11; I Cor. 2:14)?

2. Does God choose those who believe when they believe, i.e., in time, or before time (Eph. 1:4)? Did God choose (elect) those who believe because He foresaw that they would believe in Jesus Christ of their own will, or because He ordained (appointed) them to believe through the gospel before time began according to the good pleasure of His own will (Acts 13:48; Eph. 1:5-12; II Tim. 1:9)?

3. If Christ died a substitutionary atonement for the guilt and penalty of everyone's sins without exception, how can anyone be condemned to hell for his or her sins (Matt. 1:21; Mark 10:45; Rom. 8:32-34; Gal. 3:13; Rom. 8:1)?

4. Is anyone able to come to Christ by his or her own will (John 6:44)? By whose will is one born again, man's or God's (John 1:12-13; 5:40; 6:64; James 1:18)?

5. If by the death of Christ, God graciously justifies (Rom. 3:24) by faith (Rom. 5:1) those whom He calls according to His eternal purpose (Rom. 8:28; II Tim. 1:9), who can separate them from His love, which is in Christ Jesus their Lord (Rom. 8:33-39)? Who can resist the will of God or ask Him: "Why do You choose certain ones to be saved and purpose to pass by others before they have had an opportunity to do good or evil?" (Dan. 4:35; Isa. 46:9-11; Matt. 11:26; Rom. 9:11, 18-21)

CHAPTER II

PROOF FOR DEFINITE ATONEMENT FROM THE LOVE
AND ETERNAL PURPOSE OF GOD

The Attribute of Divine Love

God's love—the moving cause of redemption

Consistent with His justice, the Scripture teaches that the atonement of Christ is ultimately traced to its source in the free, sovereign, distinguishing love of God (John 3:16; Rom. 5:8; 8:31, 32).[1] In discussing the love of God, Reformed theologians frequently describe it as an aspect of the attribute of God's goodness,[2] the other aspects being His grace and mercy (some also include God's longsuffering as another aspect).

The goodness or love of God is manifested toward His creatures in a general and special way. When manifested toward His creatures in general, the love of God is the exercise of kindness toward all His creatures as creatures. This aspect of God's love is non-redemptive. Therefore, it is referred to theologically as the general love of God. When the goodness or love of God is manifested toward His creatures in a special way, it is reflected only in those whom He has loved with an everlasting love. This aspect of His love is redemptive. Therefore, it is referred to theologically as the distinguishing or redemptive love of God. It is this unalterable love of the triune God, which adds warmth of personality and a personal love to the eternal purpose and plan of God (cf. the following subheading).

God's love—immutable and distinguishing

In accordance with God's pure and holy nature, His love neither changes nor is subject to natural passions, such as man's,

---

[1] Cf. John Murray, *Redemption Accomplished and Applied* (Grand Rapids: Wm. B. Eerdmans Publishing Company, 1955), 9.

[2] Cf. William G. T. Shedd, *Dogmatic Theology* (Grand Rapids: Zondervan Publishing House, 1969; reprint of 1888 ed.), 1:385.

for "God is not a man, that he should lie" (Num. 23:19). The doctrine of a universal saving love (a general benevolence and propensity in God) for the redemptive good of all mankind without exception is entirely out of accord with the Scripture, because it logically ascribes imperfection to God. For, upon reflection, does not a natural affection in God for the good and salvation of all mankind without exception (which is never completed or perfected) carry along with it a great deal of imperfection and weakness? Certainly it does. That is why the Bible reveals that there are different manifestations of divine love. It teaches that there is a non-redemptive, general benevolence directed, in providence, toward all mankind as the creatures of God. But, it also teaches that there is a special redemptive love of God directed, in regenerating grace, toward all those whom He has "chosen" in Christ "before the foundation of the world" (Eph. 1:4). This love of God is a sacrificial love which is the highest expression of personal love, for "greater love hath no man than this, that a man lay down his life for his friends" (John 15:13). Even more, Christ died for the ungodly (Rom. 5:8; cf. John 3:16; Rom. 8:32; 1 John 3:16; 4:1-10). The intent under this subheading, therefore, is not to discuss the natural propensity or general, non-redemptive love of God for the whole of humankind, but to discuss the special discriminating love, "a love that elects and predestinates"[3] some of humankind unto eternal life according to the free and sovereign good pleasure of His infinitely wise and holy will (cf. Eph. 1:5, 9, 11).

It should be evident from Scripture that God does not manifest the same uniform affection or goodness toward all mankind, as Arminian unlimited redemptionists claim. One only has to provide one scriptural illustration, contextually cited, to prove this. For example, "Jacob have I loved, but Esau have I hated" (Rom. 9:13). To say that Christ's sacrificial death, which is the

---

[3]Murray, *Redemption*, 10.

highest expression of divine love to man, applies equally to all without exception and then observe that a multitude of mankind has and is entering a Christless eternity certainly does not magnify God's love or His wisdom. Will God love those who are in hell equally with the redeemed who are with Christ in eternity? Certainly not! A love of such design cannot be that love of God which is immutable and eternal. What kind of God is it who delivers up His Son to die for the redemption of each and every individual of mankind, yet does not send multitudes the gospel to acquaint them with the gift of salvation, or send them His Spirit to apply the benefit of redemption, or give them saving faith to lay hold upon it? Such a love would be unworthy of God and a mockery to the very persons who, according to the theory of universal redemption, were bought with Christ's blood. In effect, the universal redemptionist's view reduces to this: God loved each and every one enough to have Christ die for them, but He did not love them enough to save them, or for that matter, enough to pray for them (cf. John 17:9).

The above concept of the universal and egalitarian love of God seems infinitely more repulsive than the objections to the doctrine of particular redemption. For example, an objection is raised against saying that the love which God manifested in delivering up His only begotten Son is a special and discriminating love of God for His elect and for them alone. But to object to this is to forget that the highest form of divine love, which is the moving cause for God giving His Son to die upon the cross, is also the moving cause for imparting all the other saving graces. Does not the Scripture declare: "He that spared not his, own Son, but delivered him up for us all, how shall he not with him also freely give us all things" (Rom. 8:32)? If this is true (and it is), and if Christ died for all mankind as the universal redemptionist affirms, why is it that "all men have not faith" (II Thess. 3:2), since God has promised to freely give all things to those for whom Christ died? The immediate context in Romans 8 teaches that, among other things, predestination, calling, justification and glorification are included in the "all things" of verse 32, being expressly designed for all the Christians at Rome and, by way of extension, for all true believers. Now, if this be true (and it is), is not saving faith also included? Is one justified by any other means than faith? Not according to Scripture. Then, if the term "all" in this verse means all mankind without exception as those who believe in an indefinite atonement assert, why are not all mankind saved? The point that Paul is stressing is that those for whom God spared not his own son (i.e., those for whom Christ died, whoever they may be) are certain to be called, justified and glorified—just as certain as the fact of Christ's death on the cross. But, if "all" includes each and every individual of Adam's fallen race, then all will be saved—none will be lost. Is that what Paul is teaching? God forbid! It is concluded, therefore, that if the universal term "all" must be restricted, in this context, to God's elect who come to saving faith in time, then this term and other universal terms (e.g., "world" and "every man") must also be ultimately restricted to the same persons in those passages which refer to the crosswork of Christ (cf. John 3:16; II Cor. 5:19; Heb. 2:9; I John 2:2). Those who deny this theological interpretation are faced with a dilemma: if they reflect upon their denial, they will see that their view logically leads them to a position that contradicts itself, since the Bible also teaches that some men perish. Is this what they really believe? Undoubtedly not!

Summary

It should be apparent from the preceding polemic that only the elect of God come to the position of receiving and exercising the gift of faith. Therefore, it must be concluded that if the highest form of God's love, that love with which He "so loved the world," be the moving cause of sending Christ (and it is), it must also be the cause of all the other saving graces that are given in Christ (Rom. 8:32). Is this not true? Therefore, how can this love be intended towards any but those who have the "all things" bestowed upon them, namely, those who believe—the elect of God?

In the final analysis, the issue concerning God's love is not so much between those who hold to a definite or indefinite atonement as it is between "an effective atonement limited in breadth to the redeemed, and a universal atonement limited in depth to the point of ineffectuality."[4]

The viewpoint of the unlimited redemptionist, which demands that "world" (as it is used in such passages as John 3:16) refers to each and every individual of mankind (instead of both Jew and Gentile scattered throughout the world[5] who are ultimately manifested through faith as God's elect), logically requires this view to teach that: (1) God's love toward innumerable persons (i.e., the non-elect) is redemptively fruitless and vain; (2) the Son of God was given for innumerable individuals who never heard of Him and, even more, who had no ability given to them to believe in Him; (3) God is mutable in His love, unless He still loves those that be in hell; (4) God does not give all things to them for whom He gives His Son, which is contrary to Romans 8:32. Certainly, then, it is not only unscriptural, but illogical to say that God purposed and exercised the same sacrificial love toward all of His creatures—to the reprobate and to those chosen in Christ "before the foundation of the world" (Eph. 1:4).

The Eternal Purpose of God

The eternal purpose of God described

The eternal saving purpose of God in salvation is brought to pass in the fulness of time through the blood of Jesus Christ who is "the mediator of the new covenant" (Heb. 12:24; cf. Eph. 1:7).

---

[4]Roger Nicole, "The Case for Definite Atonement," *Bulletin of the Evangelical Theological Society,* X, no. 4 (1967), 203.

[5]For a thorough biblical study on the meaning of the term "world," the reader is referred to: John Owen, *The Death of Death in the Death of Christ* (reprint ed.; London: The Banner of Truth Trust, 1963), 205-17.

The eternal salvation of those God chose in Christ "before the foundation of the world" (Eph. 1:4) is "according to His own purpose and grace" (II Tim 1:9).[6] The accomplishment of this salvation is according to God's eternal purpose which He brings to pass "in the dispensation of the fulness of times" (Eph. 1:10), that is, in the New Covenant. God works "all things" according to "the counsel of His own will" (Eph. 1:11)—according to His "eternal purpose"—to the end that most fully manifests His wisdom, the salvation of "the church," namely, in purposing "that the Gentiles should be fellow heirs [with the Jews}, and of the same body, and partakers of His promise in Christ by the gospel" (Eph. 3:6).

The unity of the Godhead in the eternal purpose

It is essential to understand that the will of the Father will be done on earth as it is in heaven (Matt. 6:10). At the heart of God, who "works all things after the counsel of his will" (Eph. 1:11) is the triune God's plan of redemption which is accomplished "to the glory of his grace" (Eph. 1:14). The theological significance of redemption is clearly taught in Ephesians 1:3-14. There, it is distinguished from the standpoint of redemption planned by God the Father, redemption accomplished by God the Son, and redemption applied by God the Holy Spirit.

Regarding *for whom did Christ die*, the New Testament explicitly teaches the unity of purpose of the triune God in redemption. This means that Christ must have died specially for those "whom the Father had given him." For Christ to die for more than the Father had given Him would be for Christ to fail to "do always those things that please him" (John 8:29) and to seek His own will contrary to "the will of the Father which hath sent me" (John 5:30; cf. Heb. 10:7). Therefore, to say that Christ's

---

[6]Notice that II Tim. 1:9 does not call God's "eternal purpose and grace" a "*covenant of grace*" or "*covenant of redemption*" as commonly done in the theological system of Covenant Theology.

death was designed to be redemptive in the sense of actually providing salvation for all mankind without exception is to destroy the oneness between the Father and the Son (John 10:30). Furthermore, it introduces an intolerable disjunction in the divine purpose. And such a disjunction, if it were true, would threaten the unity of the trinitarian relationship "for it would show Christ intending to die for those whom the Father has not given to Him, and for those whom the Holy Spirit will not regenerate."[7] It would have Christ loving and dying for the non-elect but not loving them enough even to pray for their salvation (cf. John 17:2, 9). Yet, the Holy Spirit sovereignly regenerates only those

---

[7]Roger Nicole, "Moyse Amyraut (1596-1664) and the Controversy on Universal Grace. First Phase (1634-1637)," (unpublished Ph. D. dissertation, Department of Church History, Harvard University, 1966), 126. Douty makes a vain attempt to answer this objection by asserting that the purpose of the Godhead in the obedience and death of Christ was to "provide a complete salvation for all sinners." However, "this generous inclusion of all men in the provision made, would, because of the stubbornness of the non-elect, result in no saving benefit for them, yet it would display the goodness of God in comprehending them therein." Norman F. Douty, *The Death of Christ* (Swengel, PA: Reiner Publications, 1972), 21. But how does the provision of salvation for the non-elect display the goodness of God? Is it hypothetical or actual? If hypothetical, it is no provision at all. If actual, it would only display the goodness of God in His enduring "with much longsuffering the vessels of wrath fitted to destruction" (Rom. 9:22). But the scriptural reason for God's longsuffering toward the non-elect is not, as Douty says, that He should receive glory for "being a God generous enough to provide salvation for them" (cf. Douty, 91). The scriptural reason is that God wills to show forth "his wrath, and to make his power known" through the just condemnation of the vessels of dishonour that His "name might be declared throughout all the earth" as was God's purpose in the case of Pharaoh (cf. Rom. 9:22 in context). God's longsuffering is for the salvation of the elect, that not one of them should perish (II Pet. 3:9, 15). God's longsuffering is designed so that He "might make known the riches of his glory on the vessels of mercy, which he had afore prepared unto glory. Even us, whom he hath called not of the Jews only, but of the Gentiles" (Rom. 9:23, 24).

whom He wills (cf. John 3:8), namely, those whom the Father
chose in Christ "before the foundation of the world" (Eph. 1:4).

The universal gospel call and the eternal purpose of God

Apart from the express demands of Scripture that it is God's
will that His ambassadors go "into all the world, and preach the
gospel to every creature" (Mark 16:15), it is also a sure source of
inevitable error to overlook the purpose of God in the relationship
between the gospel call to repentance and faith and the New
Covenant. This is an important relationship because the gospel
call comes forth *from* the New Covenant and summons sinners
into it. Therefore, it must be a worldwide call. The one thing it
takes for granted is that sinners are outside the covenant. Before
God's elect are effectually called into covenant union with Christ,
they are outside the New Covenant because they are by nature
"children of wrath, even as others" (Eph. 2:3). Their identity and
election unto salvation prior to the effectual application of
Christ's wonderful redemption by the Holy Spirit is known only
to God, not to His ambassadors. Is there any inconsistency then
in God's ambassadors heralding the gospel call to all mankind
without distinction, which includes the elect who, like the non-
elect, are outside covenant relationship with Christ? Is it
inconsistent to preach the gospel to every creature, to those
outside the covenant, just because the basis for the call rests upon
grounds within the covenant? Certainly not. It has to be
accomplished this way. Could the gospel call bring sinners into
the New Covenant if the call—

> itself rested on grounds outside the covenant? Whatever is without
> the covenant, outside its limits—as an indefinite unlimited
> atonement is—has nothing to do with the gospel call; can impart to
> it no validity, no strength, no enlargement; can constitute for it no
> real basis or foundation. An indefinite atonement, therefore, as
> pleaded for by some in the interests of the freeness of the gospel

call, is one of the most self-contradictory and self-negativing devices that can be imagined.[8]

It must be remembered that, in the giving of the gospel call, preachers are only God's ambassadors—His ministers of righteousness. They give the call ministerially. The Father is the one who effectually calls by the Holy Spirit. When the Spirit gives forth the gospel call, it is a glorious exercise of God's grace, which always effectively, through the miracle of regeneration, enables a lost sinner to savingly believe in Jesus Christ and enter into the covenant of the redeemed. And the only thing which the ambassadors of the gospel call presume is that—

> sinners are not inside—not yet interested in—this blessed covenant or constitution; that they are aliens from the blessed kingdom of which it is the charter. It is, therefore, in its essential nature obviously a universal call. It is so because it is a call *to* the covenant.[9]

On the contrary, to make the gospel call proceed upon grounds broader than the New Covenant is to destroy the call of all its intrinsic worth and design. If the call is not a call to covenant union with Christ and to all of the redeemer's free grace and saving blessings, it is of no value. It is of no value if it is a call coming from any object other than from Christ as the covenant head.

Before moving to the next subheading, it should be observed that some who object to Calvinistic particularism, especially

---

[8]Hugh Martin, *The Atonement* (reprint of 1871 ed.; Cherry Hill, New Jersey: Mack Publishing Company, n.d.), 8. The reader should note that I have adapted Hugh Martin's understanding of "the covenant" from being the theologically deduced covenant of grace to the explicit scriptural teaching of the New Covenant. In my judgment this modification makes his statement applicable to New Covenant Theology's understanding that the everlasting covenant is the New Covenant not to the final covenantal administration of the "one covenant of grace" system of traditional Covenant Theology.

[9]*Ibid.*

evangelical Arminians, think that Calvinists cannot consistently preach the gospel to every creature, as set forth above, unless every creature has within himself the ability to comply. Others, such as the modified Calvinists, think that Calvinists cannot consistently proclaim the message of salvation to every creature through the worldwide gospel call unless the atonement of Christ was, in some way, made alike for all mankind—alike for those who perish and for those who are saved.[10] In brief, the *Arminians* believe the *universal gospel call* supposes universal redemption and *universal ability; the modified Calvinists* believe the *universal gospel offer* supposes *universal redemption* and *total*

---

[10]A language of double-talk is the inevitable result. For example, Douty writes that "Christ's redemptive work was primarily for the elect, and only secondarily for the rest of men. ... It was designed to make salvation *sure* [for the elect], but only *possible* [for the non-elect]. ... Thus God's intention in the death of Christ was not the same with reference to the two groups. But though God's design in Christ's death was dual, we must not think that the death itself was; for Christ did not die in one sense for the elect, and in another for the non-elect. ... So the sense in which Christ died for elect and non-elect was single, but His object in doing so was double. He aimed by His death to bring the elect infallibly to glory, but He never aimed by it to bring the non-elect there. All He purposed to do for them was to make it possible for them to get there, provided they repent and believe." (Cf. Douty, *The Death of Christ,* 49). God's design, says Douty, in Christ's death was for a twofold purpose, but the death itself was single in purpose. The sense in which Christ died for the elect and non-elect was single but the object was double. Yet, Douty adds that Christ's redemptive work was primarily for the elect and only secondarily for the non-elect; that is, Christ only aimed by His death to bring the elect to glory. Is this not a classic example of theological double-talk? The sense of God's redemptive purpose is dual, but the aim of Christ in His death is singular. How comforting! From this kind of teaching how is a lost sinner to know whether the Father purposed that Christ died for him primarily or secondarily? How can he know if the Son, by His death, aimed to bring him infallibly to glory or only to make it possible for him to get there conditioned upon his own repentance and faith? May the reader try to explain this double-talk.

inability. Both believe in an unlimited or indefinite atonement. But neither can view redemption—

> as actual deliverance from the punishment and power of sin, without being shut up to universal salvation. [So they] soon cut down the offer of the Gospel to the offer of pardon,—feeling that they cannot say of the righteousness of Christ, in its glorious fulness, of his active and passive obedience, what they say so boldly of his sufferings and death, they separate these, and cut down the ground of the Gospel offer to the death of Christ,—feeling that they cannot even say of this that it is universal in the way of a vicarious sacrifice and real satisfaction, they cut this down next, and say that the death of Christ does not secure any saving benefit to any, and is as much endured for the lost as for the saved, and, finally, feeling that any thing, whatever specific, might hamper them, they get quit of all by saying that the atonement is a great fact—a "general something"— equally done for all, but not securing saving blessings, or any blessings, to any; and as certainly, as fully, wrought out for Judas, who perished, as for Paul, who is saved.[11]

The representative principle and the eternal purpose

Romans 5:12-21 is the key passage which sets forth the representative principle involving the unique headships of Adam and Christ. Nothing short of an unbiblical Arminian or universalistic exegesis of this passage can prove that Christ died for all mankind. Once biblically proved that the "all men" of verse 18 are co-extensive, then I will concede that the doctrine of definite atonement is not in accord with the Word of God. But until this is accomplished, observe that this passage develops the parallel between Adam and Christ, Adam as the representative head of his seed—the fallen race (all mankind), and Christ as the representative head of His seed—the redeemed race (God's

---

[11]John Bonar, "The Universal Calls and Invitations of the Gospel Consistent with the Total Depravity of Man, and Particular Redemption," *The Banner of Truth,* 14th Issue (February, 1959), 17.

elect). Adam and Christ are unique representative heads. Verse 18 teaches that—

> on account of the offence of Adam, the sentence of death was pronounced upon all whom he represented. On account of the righteousness of Jesus Christ, the sentence of justification unto life was pronounced in favour of all whom He represented.[12]

A contextual interpretation of this passage will establish that the "many" of verse 18, with reference to Adam, must theologically include all his seed, and the "many," with respect to Christ, must theologically include all His seed. Therefore, it may be concluded that Romans 5:12-21 teaches "that the principles upon which sin and misery came upon the race through Adam are identical with those upon which righteousness and blessedness come upon the elect through Christ."[13]

False views concerning the relation of Adam and the effect that his representativeship had upon the entire human race must inevitably produce false views concerning the representativeship of Christ and the triune God's intended design in the work of redemption. The doctrine of substitutionary atonement based upon Christ's penal satisfaction for the guilt and penalty of the elect's sins is biblically and doctrinally grounded upon the representative principle set forth in Romans 5:12-21.[14] Just as the first Adam by his disobedience in his first sin represented all

---

[12]Robert Haldane, *Exposition of the Epistle to the Romans* (London: The Banner of Truth Trust, 1963), 217.

[13]Loraine Boettner *Studies in Theology* (6th ed.; Philadelphia: The Presbyterian and Reformed Publishing Company, 1964), 315.

[14]In orthodox Christianity, two views termed "realistic union" and "representative union" are set forth to theologically explain the true nature of the solidaric union of Adam's first sin with his posterity. Personally, I hold to the representative union view. Cf. my "Doctrine of Original Sin in New England Theology: From Jonathan Edwards to Edwards Amasa Park" (unpublished Th. D. dissertation, Dallas Theological Seminary, 1972), 32, 239-40.

mankind as their covenant head, so by obedience in life and death the last Adam, Christ, represented all the redeemed race as their covenant head. By the one act of transgression of the first Adam, all his seed are legally constituted as guilty sinners when they come into existence by virtue of their representative union with him. By the obedience of the last Adam, all His seed are legally constituted as righteous at conversion by virtue of their representative union with Him.

The eternal purpose and the salvation of the elect

In the temporal realm, the first distinction between the seed of the woman and the seed of the serpent (Gen. 3:15) is enough to overthrow the alleged universalism in God's saving purpose. For who would affirm that God entered into a covenant with the seed of the serpent? Singularly, the seed of the woman refers to Christ Himself (Gal. 3:16) and collectively to His elect who are the saved of all ages, the spiritual seed of Abraham (Gal. 3:28-29). Fulfillment of God's saving purpose is manifested throughout history by the efficacious calling and regeneration of the seed of the woman, the Messianic or covenantal line. The covenantal line is clearly evident in the Abrahamic, Davidic and New Covenants, which are the historical outworkings of God's eternal purpose in the history of salvation.

The seed of the serpent is manifested in Scripture near the end of the Old Testament dispensation in the words of the Lord when He told the reprobate Pharisees, "ye are of your father the devil" (John 8:44), and "ye believe not, because ye are not of my sheep" (John 10:26).

The writer of the Epistle to the Hebrews makes it clear that Christ (with a view to save) "took on him the seed of Abraham" (2:16), not (with a view to save) the seed of the serpent. The context of chapter 2 makes it abundantly clear that the flesh and blood which Christ took part of is the same as that of "the children which God hath given" Him (vv. 13, 14). And are not these the brethren of verse 11, "who are sanctified" and "for which cause he is not ashamed to call them brethren"? Are not these also the "many sons" of verse 10, which "by the grace of God he should taste death for" (v. 9)?

The teaching of the above Scripture and a multitude of other passages which contain the same truth should establish that the covenantal line is Abraham's spiritual seed. Is it not true that "if ye be Christ's, then are ye Abraham's seed and heirs according to the promise" (Gal. 3:29)? "Now to Abraham and his seed were the promises" of God made (Gal. 3:16); that "the blessing of Abraham might come on the Gentiles through Jesus Christ; that we might receive the promise of the Spirit through faith" (Gal. 3:14). The covenant with Abraham was confirmed "before of God in Christ" (Gal. 3:17), and "no man disannulleth, or addeth thereto" (Gal. 3:15). And it is with these covenant ones and to them alone that "the Son of man is come to seek and to save" (Luke 19:10). Was not the "woman which had a spirit of infirmity" (Luke 13:11) a "daughter of Abraham" (Luke 13:16), and was not Zacchaeus "a son of Abraham" (Luke 19:9)? Are not the ones called out by God in this present dispensation the spiritual seed of Abraham (Gal. 3:29), and are they "not of the Jews only, but also of the Gentiles" (Rom. 9:24; cf. Isa. 49:6)?

Does not the Old Testament Scripture teach that the Father promised the Son a reward for His sufferings? Does it not teach that, when Christ "shalt make his soul an offering for sin, he shall see his seed" (Isa. 53:10), that "he shall see of the travail of his soul and shall be satisfied" (Isa. 53:11), all because it is determined that God's righteous Servant "should justify many" (Isa. 53:10-12)?

Now the sum of the above can be reinforced by asking two questions of the Arminians. First, how could it be certain that Christ should "see his seed" and "see of the travail of his soul and be satisfied" unless the salvation of certain members of mankind had been divinely decreed and, therefore, sure to be saved? Second, how could it be certain that Christ should "justify many" if no effectual provision was made that any should receive Him as Saviour? Will not only those who are ordained to eternal life believe (Acts 13:48)? The answers should be obvious. But the Arminian, if consistent in his position, has to deny the certainty of salvation because it is contingent upon the free choice of man. To insist that the Lord Jesus did expressly purpose to provide salvation for all mankind is to charge Him with—

> that which no intelligent being should be guilty of, namely, to design that which by virtue of His omniscience He knew would never come to pass. Hence the only alternative left us is that, so far as the pre-determined purpose of His death is concerned, Christ died for the elect only.[15]

The conclusion must be that Christ did not die to make possible the salvation of all mankind, which includes both the seed of the serpent and the seed of the woman. But the conclusion must be that Christ died to make certain the salvation of all that the Father had given Him. Although the modified Calvinist agrees with this conclusion in reference to the elect, he extends the purpose of God in the atonement to include a provisional redemption for the non-elect, basing his theological position, essentially, on three verses of Scripture (II Pet. 2:1; I John 2:2; and, II Cor. 5:19).[16]

For those who believe in total depravity (i.e., the total inability of man to savingly please God out of innate ability), it should be obvious that the elect are the spiritual seed of Abraham, the seed of the woman, who are none other than "the children of God that were scattered abroad" (John 11:52). And it should follow that, "if God purposed that the elect should certainly be saved, and others left to the just consequences of their sins, Christ *could not* have designed the benefits of his death indifferently for all

---

[15]Arthur W. Pink, *The Sovereignty of God* (British rev. ed.; London: The Banner of Truth Trust, 1961), 57.

[16]Cf. Appendixes I-III of this work for a more extensive discussion of these verses.

men."[17] Therefore, does not the election of God support the doctrine of definite atonement rather than indefinite atonement? Certainly it does. It is concluded, therefore, that only the doctrine of definite atonement is consistent with the scriptural doctrine that God has from eternity sovereignly elected certain persons to eternal life and to all the means thereof.

The eternal purpose and reprobation

The purpose of God in reprobation is seen in the relationship which the seed of the serpent has with the seed of the woman. The seed of the serpent are the non-elect, reprobate—those who are destined to depart this world in a final state of unbelief. That they are Satan's seed is seen in the words of the omniscient Lord when He calls the reprobate Pharisees, "ye serpents, ye generation of vipers, how can ye escape the damnation of hell" (Matt. 23:33), or tells them "ye are of your father the devil, and the lusts of your father ye will do" (John 8:44). Do not these verses teach the truth of Genesis 3:15, namely, that there is to be perpetual enmity exercised by the seed of the serpent against the seed of the woman? Are not the reprobate the ones to whom Christ will say, "I never knew you: depart from me, ye that work iniquity" (Matt. 7:23)? But is it not strange that Christ should die for them and redeem those that He will not own, professing He never knew them? Therefore, it must be that—

> Christ died for no more than God promised unto him that he should die for. But God did not promise him to all, as that he should die for them; for he did not promise the seed of the woman to the seed of the serpent, Christ to reprobates. ... In sum, the seed of the woman died not for the seed of the serpent."[18]

It should also be acknowledged that, theologically, the essential nature of the great transaction of the atonement does not

---

[17]Archibald Alexander Hodge, *Outlines of Theology*, (1879 rev. ed.; London: The Banner of Truth Trust, 1972), 418.

[18]Owen, *The Death of Death in the Death of Christ*, 179.

depend upon the time of its accomplishment. "It would be a real propitiation for the sins of all who should ever take him as their surety, were it yet to be accomplished."[19] Conversely, is it possible that Christ intended in His death to satisfy for the sins of all and every reprobate already in hell?

> Shall we suppose that Christ would make himself an offering for their sins whom he knew to be past recovery? ... Shall we think that the blood of the covenant was cast away upon them for whom our Saviour intended no good at all? To intend good to them he could not, without a direct opposition to the eternal decree of His Father, and therein of his own eternal Deity. Did God send his Son, did Christ come to die, for Cain and Pharaoh, damned so many ages before his suffering?[20]

Yet, this must be the case if the atonement is unlimited in extent. Concerning this point, Spurgeon preached:

> If Christ on His cross intended to save every man, then He intended to save those who were lost before He died. If the doctrine be true, that He died for all men, then He died for some who were in Hell before He came into this world, for doubtless there were even then myriads there who had been cast away because of their sins. ... [This] seems to me a conception a thousand times more repulsive than any of those consequences which are said to be associated with the Calvinistic and Christian doctrine of special and particular redemption. To think that my Saviour died for men who were or are in hell, seems a supposition too horrible for me to entertain.[21]

Summary

The redemptive plan of God is manifested chiefly through the historical outworkings of the eternal purpose of a loving, merciful, covenant-keeping God. The motivating cause behind

---

[19]Robert S. Candlish, *The Atonement* (Edinburgh: Adam and Charles Black, 1867), 351.

[20]Owen, *The Death of Death in the Death of Christ,* 136.

[21]Charles Haddon Spurgeon, *The Early Years* (rev. ed.; London: The Banner of Truth Trust, 1962), 172.

God's plan of redemption is His special distinguishing love. It is those who are chosen in Christ "before the foundation of the world" (Eph. 1:4) that God, "according to the good pleasure of his will" (Eph. 1:5), sent and gave His Son as a surety to save (Rom. 8:32). And His ultimate purpose is designed for "the praise of the glory of his grace, wherein he hath made us accepted in the beloved [One]" (Eph. 1:6).

Central to the fulfillment of His eternal purpose in redemptive history is the elect's union with Christ. Concerning the nature of this elective union between Christ and His people, one of America's leading theologians asserted that the Bible teaches:

(1) That a certain portion of the human race were given to Christ. (2) That they were given to Him before the foundation of the world. (3) That all thus given to Him will certainly come to Him and be saved. (4) That this union, so far as it was from eternity, is not a union of nature, nor by faith, nor by the indwelling of the Holy Spirit. It was a federal union.[22] (5) That Christ, therefore, was a federal head and representative. As such He came into the world, and all He did and suffered was as a representative, as a substitute, one acting in place

---

[22]However, it should be noted that *federal union* although rightly distinguished should not be *separated* from *experiential, spiritual union* (see Murray, *Redemption*, 161-173). Further, it should be noted that *federal union* as explained by Hodge and most Reformed theologians also refers to a pre-fall *covenant of works* that God made with Adam. I believe that a pre-fall covenant relationship between God and Adam was necessary for Adam to be the unique representative head of all mankind (Rom. 5:12-19). However, I believe that the *covenant of works* explanation is flawed in teaching that Adam would have earned (?) *eternal* life if he had continued to obey God's commandment not to eat of the forbidden fruit for an unspecified probationary period. For Adam, obedience may have resulted in perpetual *earthly* life, but *eternal* life, no! Heaven had to come down! Heaven had to come down according to God's eternal purpose and grace in the person and work of Christ for man to receive *eternal* life (II Tim. 1:9). In brief, for purpose of this footnote, I believe that Reformed Theology's *covenant of works—covenant of grace* teaching has some major theological weaknesses as classically set forth, e.g., in the Westminster Confession of Faith and the Second London Baptist Confession of 1689.

and for the benefit of others. But He was the representative of those given to Him, i.e., of those who were in Him. For it was this gift and the union consequent upon it, that gave Him his representative character, or constituted Him a federal head. He was therefore the federal head, not of the human race, but of those given to Him by the Father. And, therefore, his work, so far as its main design is concerned, was for them alone.[23]

The fulfillment of the promise of an everlasting covenant (Isa. 61:8) in the New Covenant oneness of Christ with His people is the basis for the Lord saying, "this is the Father's will which hath sent me, that of all which he hath given me I should lose nothing" (John 6:39). Yet, if Christ died a substitutionary death for all mankind, how and why is it that He loses a multitude of them? Does not the Scripture declare that "he doeth according to his will in the army of heaven, and among the inhabitants of the earth: and none can stay his hand" (Dan. 4:35); or again, "Lo, I come to do thy will, 0 God" (Heb. 10:7, 9)?

Therefore, it is concluded that because of God's eternal purpose and grace (II Tim. 1:9) redemption was accomplished through the blood of the everlasting covenant (Heb. 13:20), the New Covenant in Christ. Further, it is concluded that Christ did not die equally or provisionally for all mankind, rather He died as a substitutionary ransom for His people, those chosen in Him "before the foundation of the world" (Eph. 1:4), and for them alone.

---

[23]Charles Hodge, *Systematic Theology* (Grand Rapids: Wm. B. Eerdmans Publishing Company, n.d.; reprint of the 1871-1873 ed.), 2:551.

For Whom Did Christ Die?

"God imposed His wrath due unto, and the Son underwent the pains of hell for, either:

1. All the sins of all men, or
2. All the sins of some men, or
3. Some sins of all men.

If the last, some sins of all men, then all men have some sins to answer for, and so no man shall be saved.

If the second, that is it which we affirm, that Christ in their stead ... suffered for all the sins of all the elect in the world.

If the first, why, then, are not all freed from the punishment of all their sins?

You will say, 'Because of their unbelief; they will not believe.' But this unbelief, is it a sin, or not? If not, why should they be punished for it? If it be, then Christ underwent the punishment due unto it, or not. If so, then why must that hinder them more than their other sins for which He died? ... If He did not, then He did not die for all their sins." (John Owen, c. 1650)

CHAPTER III

PROOF FOR DEFINITE ATONEMENT FROM THE REDEMPTIVE WORK OF CHRIST

General

The controversy with regard to the extent of the atonement does not reside, as most unlimited redemptionists would have it, in the infinite sufficiency of Christ's sufferings and merits. Rather the controversy resides in the purpose, design or intent of God in inflicting sufferings and death upon His Son and of Christ in voluntarily submitting to them. Therefore, unlimited redemptionists, whether Arminians or modified Calvinists, must seek to indicate and prove that God in some way purposed, designed or actually intended to provide salvation for all mankind without exception.

> And for the Calvinistic universalists to assert the existence of such a purpose, design, or intention ... requires the introduction of a good deal of confusion and ambiguity into their mode of stating and arguing the case. They cannot say, with the Arminians, that Christ died equally for all men; for they cannot dispute that God's special purpose of grace in regard to the elect ... must have, in some sense and to some extent, regulated or influenced the whole of the process by which God's purpose was accomplished,—by which His decree of election was executed.[1]

Therefore, the Calvinistic universalists contend that there was a twofold purpose to the atonement—one general for all mankind; one special for the elect only. In doing this they separate the finished work of Christ in His sacrifice from the application of it by the Holy Spirit. To illustrate, one contemporary modified Calvinist has written:

> The personal application of the finished work has nothing to do with the completeness of the work. In fact, the accomplishments of

---

[1]William Cunningham, *Historical Theology*, 4th ed. (London: The Banner of Truth Trust, 1960), 2:334

Christ on the cross are complete and final even if no one had ever appropriated their benefits.[2]

More will be stated concerning the application of the atonement by the Spirit of God in Chapter IV. However, for the present, this chapter will discuss the importance that the priestly ministry of Christ has in proving the doctrine of definite atonement. The primary design of the following discussion of Christ's priestly ministry is to establish that both Christ's sacrifice and intercession are co-extensive and inseparable from His priestly office. The secondary design of this chapter (supplemented by Appendixes I-III) is to establish that Christ's priestly ministry is not compatible with the major theological proofs for unlimited atonement as asserted by the modified Calvinists.

Christ in His Priestly Office

Introduction

The redemptive work of Christ should not be discussed apart from Christ's priestly action in His death. It is in the priestly office of Christ that the infinitely important subject of Christ's atonement is to be discussed. It is this office of Christ that the Father ratified with an immutable oath for "the Lord hath sworn, and will not repent, Thou are a priest for ever after the order of Melchizedek" (Ps. 110:4; cf. Heb. 5:6; 6:20; 7:17, 21). And it was in this office that the Father glorified the Son "to be made a high priest" (Heb. 5:5). Therefore, Christ's priesthood must be regarded and set forth as pre-eminently the foundational office which Christ as a redeemer executes. It was Socinus and his followers (cf. Note No. 5, Appendix III) who first regarded Christ's priestly office as separate from His sufferings and death, as not being executed at all upon earth, but only after His ascension to heaven. In effect, the Socinians equated Christ's

---

[2]Robert P. Lightner, *The Death Christ Died-A Case for Unlimited Atonement* (Des Plaines, Illinois: Regular Baptist Press, 1967), 96.

intercession in heaven with the entirety of His priestly ministry. It is an offspring of this heresy which has unknowingly permeated the teachings of many evangelicals today who hold to universal redemption. As a result, it has caused them (as frequently reflected in their writings) to obscure Christ's priestly office by representing His death as a suffering instead of that which He actively achieved. I have yet to find a work by an unlimited redemptionist which sets forth proof for unlimited atonement under a heading relating to Christ's priestly office.

Without hesitation, the defenders of unlimited redemption, or an indefinite atonement, interpret the three important doctrinal words—redemption, propitiation and reconciliation—in a twofold sense to avoid universal salvation. As a result, they separate the purchase of Christ (which is for all) from its application (which is for some). A detailed discussion of these three doctrinal words is contained in Appendixes I-III. But, for the present, it should be observed that, to make the atonement indefinite and universal, the sacrifice of Christ is said to *"provide redemption, reconciliation and propitiation for all men"*[3]—to make it "possible" for all men to be saved.[4] But this only results in a removal of legal obstacles (bars) for the non-elect—not a penal substitution. That this is true is clearly evidenced in evangelical, modified Calvinistic, nineteenth and twentieth century writings. For example, one recent modified Calvinist wrote that "the sin of the world [all mankind] is taken away in the sense that by Christ's threefold accomplishment [redemption, propitiation and reconciliation] in His death every hindrance is removed."[5] But, if one were to ask a modified Calvinist: "Did Christ die to remove legal bars?"—he would say, "No, He

---

[3] *Ibid.*, 146.

[4] *Ibid.*, 47.

[5] Lewis Sperry Chafer, *Systematic Theology* (Dallas: Dallas Seminary Press, 1948), 5:191.

removed legal bars by dying." And this is all that is necessary to show that the unlimited redemptionist, if consistent, should speak of result and not mere "possibility" in the sacrifice of Christ. But this he does not do. However, is it not the clear teaching of Scripture that the result of Christ's death was the obtaining of "eternal redemption for us" (Heb. 9:12), not the mere removal of bars? Some openly assert that the removal of legal bars was all that Christ's redemption did for the non-elect, but that it was both a removal of the legal hindrances and a substitution for the elect.[6] But of what value is this? It only forms a basis for saying there is a redemption which does not redeem.

What was the extent of Christ's redemptive work in His death? The proof of what He did is evidenced in the end result, namely, in the salvation of those that believe. But what is the mere "removal of bars"? It is not substitutionary. Ultimately, it proves to be only hypothetical. Consequently, it seems to be a mockery of God's wisdom, for it recognizes no results and degrades Christ's priesthood.

The qualifications for a high priest

"Every high priest taken from among men is ordained for men in things pertaining to God, that he may offer both gifts and sacrifices for sins" (Heb. 5:1). This Scripture sets forth the qualifications for a high priest. First, the high priest must possess the nature and be related to the race for whose welfare he mediates. This Christ did when—

> he took not on *him the nature* of angels; but he took on *him* the seed of Abraham. Wherefore in all things it behooved him to be made like unto *his* brethren, that he might be a merciful and faithful high priest in things *pertaining* to God, to make reconciliation [propitiation] for the sins of the people (Heb. 2:16,17).

---

[6]Ralph Wardlaw, *Systematic Theology* (Edinburgh: Adam and Charles Black, 1857), 2:438-83.

Second, a high priest must possess the call and ordination of God. This was true of Christ. He was ordained "with an oath by" the Lord who "sware and will not repent, Thou art a priest for ever after the order of Melchisedec" (Heb. 7:21).

Third, a high priest must make offering to God for a people and not for God to a people. This Christ did when He, "through the eternal Spirit offered himself without spot to God" (Heb. 9:14), "that he might be a merciful and faithful high priest in things pertaining to God, to make reconciliation [propitiation] for the sins of the people" (Heb. 2:17).

Fourth, the offering of the high priest must be for sins. This Christ did "once, when he offered up himself" (Heb. 7:27) and "bare our sins in his own body on the tree" (I Pet. 2:24). Note that His offering was not for "sin" in the abstract and impersonal, but for "sins." His offering was for actual and individual sins—for those of the people for whom He died.

Combine Christ's fulfillment of the qualifications for His high priesthood with His spotless personal holiness and His perpetual intercession, and one has the full doctrine of the priesthood of Christ. And within it the doctrine of the atonement is revealed—a doctrine which cannot be separated from it without being shorn of its glory and left almost defenseless. For, if the atonement of Christ falls under the category of His priesthood,

> ... it is impossible [for it to] be impersonal, indefinite, unlimited; for the priesthood is not. In order to its very constitution, it prerequires personal relation; and the same must be true of the Atonement, unless the Atonement transpires outside the limits and actings and conditions of the priesthood. The priesthood is "for men," and for "sins." Not for mankind in the general, but "for *men,*"—particular men. And not for *sin* in the general, but "for sins,"—particular sins. The personal relation of the priest is a relation to particular persons, with especial reference to their particular sins; or,

more briefly, it is a relation to these persons considered as sinners. A general reference or relation is out of the question.[7]

Therefore, it is concluded that the introduction of an unlimited reference into the priestly office of Christ is without foundation. It is without foundation, first, because it is not a fulfillment of the Old Testament typical sacrifices; and, second, because the writer of Hebrews makes it evident that Christ's sacrifice and intercession are co-extensive for a definite people. The proof of the former is found in Hebrews 10:14, "by one offering he [Christ] hath perfected for ever them that are sanctified." The proof of the latter is found in Hebrews 7:25, "Wherefore he is able also to save them to the uttermost that come unto God by him, seeing he ever liveth to make intercession for them."

Furthermore, an unlimited reference into the priestly office of Christ violates the qualifications of the kinsman-redeemer concept. The four qualifications for a kinsman-redeemer are that he must: (1) be a near kinsman (close relative); (2) be able to accomplish the redemption; (3) be willing to redeem; (4) accomplish the redemption. Yet, if an unlimited reference is introduced into the priestly office, it would make Christ the near kinsman of the seed of the serpent, and it would have required him to be willing to redeem them for whom the Father had not willed to give Him. In addition, the fourth qualification cannot be met at all unless one is willing to hold to universal salvation. The universal redemptionist attempts to get around this problem by saying that Christ died not to *accomplish* redemption for all mankind, but only to *provide* it for all mankind. But, does not this completely eliminate the fourth qualification for a kinsman redeemer? What kind of a redeemer is it who does not accomplish redemption?

---

[7]Hugh Martin, *The Atonement* (reprint of 1871 ed.; Cherry Hill, New Jersey: Mack Publishing Company, n.d.), 31.

The priestly sacrifice of Christ

General.—Many fail to see the sacrifice of Christ as a priestly work on earth. Therefore, the first object under this subheading will be to establish this aspect of Christ's priestly ministry. All who are orthodox in their beliefs hold that the supreme significance of Christ's sacrifice was its substitutionary nature, although many logically deny it in effect when they insist that Christ died for all mankind without exception. Therefore, as a second object under this subheading, it will be demonstrated that the penal substitutionary nature of Christ's atonement is consistent only with a definite atonement. Third, I have digressed somewhat from the predominantly positive approach by referring the reader to a discussion of three doctrinal words in Appendixes I-III concerning the sacrifice of Christ. This divergence is important because out of all the effects or benefits of Christ's death, which a born-again believer receives, only three are said by unlimited redemptionists to extend to those who never believe, the non-elect. They are redemption, propitiation and reconciliation.

On earth.—From the qualifications for a high priest, as set forth above, it was established that Christ offered Himself as a sacrifice for the sins of a definite people and that this offering was in execution of His priestly office. This in itself should be enough to prove that it had to be on earth. But to affirm this truth further, let the reader note that Ephesians 5:2 definitely teaches that Christ served as a high priest while on earth. It states that Christ "loved us, and hath given himself for us an offering and a sacrifice to God" (cf. Heb. 5:1-4). And this sacrifice is the same "once for all" offering of Hebrews 10:10. No sacrifice of Christ other than that which He offered on the earth can be said to be once offered. That which is done in heaven is done always, eternally, and cannot be said to be done "once for all." Further proof that it was a priestly sacrifice that was made on earth is found in Hebrews 1:3; 5:6,7; 7:27; 9:26; 10:10,12,14; I Peter 2:24.

A penal substitution.—It is held by all who are of the orthodox faith that Christ's death was a penal substitution for sinners. But the difference between those who hold to a definite and an indefinite atonement is found in the general statements and disputed passages of Scripture which the universal redemptionist says teach an unlimited substitution of a twofold character. Since both adherents claim to base their doctrine upon Scripture, the answer, ideally, lies in that doctrine which is consistent with a combined and harmonious interpretation of all the passages bearing upon the subject. It is impossible within the scope of this work to examine every passage. But, except for John 3:16 (which was briefly treated under the first major subheading of Chapter II and will be discussed somewhat further in Appendix II as it relates to I John 2:2), there are three key verses admitted by the modified Calvinists which are central to proving their doctrine of unlimited atonement. The verses are II Peter 2:1 (which pertains to redemption), I John 2:2 (which pertains to propitiation), and II Corinthians 5:19 (which pertains to reconciliation). These three verses are discussed in detail in Appendixes I-III, respectively.

The doctrine of definite atonement possesses a great advantage over the doctrine of indefinite atonement in harmonizing the whole of Scripture. There are a number of reasons for saying this. First, that Scripture which explicitly teaches a doctrine (such as the teaching on the extent of the atonement in Isa. 53; John 10 and 17) takes precedence over such passages which do not explicitly teach the same doctrine but some other doctrine or aspect of divine truth. (For example, John 3:16 does not stress the quantitative nature but the qualitative nature of God's love.) Furthermore, it is much easier to understand and explain why general or indefinite language may have been used when absolute universality was not meant than to explain why limited or definite language should ever have been used if the atonement was designed for all mankind without exception.

Second, there are scriptural statements (some of which have already been set forth and some of which will follow) which cannot, by any fair process of interpretation, be reconciled with the doctrine of universal redemption.

Third, in the context of every passage where Christ is spoken of as dying for the "world," "all," or "every," there is contextual evidence for asserting that the universal terms are not to be understood as absolute for all mankind. Rather it can be scripturally demonstrated that, in these passages which use universal terms, the object is—

> to indicate merely that those for whom Christ died are not confined to any one nation, class, or description of men,-the world, or the whole world, evidently meaning mankind at large, Gentiles as well as Jews, a truth which it was then peculiarly necessary to enforce, and to bring out in the fullest and strongest terms, in consequence of the abuse made of the selection of the Jews as God's peculiar people.[8]

Fourth, I am persuaded that most unlimited redemptionists have not examined the subject with care or with scriptural objectivity and are, for the most part, either ignorant or ignore the context of the Scripture and the teachings of the great reformation divines concerning this doctrine. For example, there is a noticeable lack among the writings of unlimited redemptionists of any attempt to prove their contention that "world" in the disputed passages always means "world," namely, all mankind without exception. This meaning is invariably assumed by them when they comment concerning the extent of the atonement.

Fifth, if Christ has truly borne the sins of all men in penal substitution, there is nothing left for divine justice to punish.[9] The logic of universal substitution would therefore imply universal

---

[8]Cunningham, *Historical Theology,* 2:341.

[9]For an answer to those who say penal substitution is conditioned on faith, see Chapter IV of this work.

salvation. "But salvation will be restricted to some only of the race: redemption and substitution must therefore be particular as well, or redemption must be in some other way than by substitution."[10]

Sixth, it is the same love of God to men, the same death of Christ and the same ransom price paid for men that is connected both with the definite and the indefinite phraseology. God loved the world, and Christ loved His church; Christ died for all, and He died for His sheep; He gave Himself a ransom for all, and He gave Himself a ransom for many. Therefore, there can be—

> no warrant whatever for alleging that, in the one case, the love, and the ransom are descriptive of totally different things from what they describe in the other. The very same things are predicated of the two classes, the all and the sheep, the all and the many; and, *therefore, the fair inference is, that they are not really two different classes, but one and the same class,* somewhat differently described, and ... regarded under somewhat different aspects.[11]

It should not be ignored that the Scripture emphasizes the definite relation of the mission of Christ in His sacrificial death for those whom He actually redeems. Nicole makes this point when he states:

> Christ gave Himself for His people (Mt. 1:21), for His friends (John 15:13), for His sheep (John 10:15), for His church (Eph. 5:23-26; Acts 20:28), for many (Mt. 20:28; 26:28; Mk. 10:45), for us (Tit. 2:14), for me (Gal. 2:20). These expressions need not be construed as exclusive of others not explicitly mentioned—(this is quite manifest in the case of Gal. 2:20)—but the specific reference in all these passages certainly indicates that the relationship of the

[10]Roger Nicole, "Moyse Amyraut (1596-1664) and the Controversy on Universal Grace. First Phase (1634-1637)," (unpublished Ph.D. dissertation, Department of Church History, Harvard University, 1966), 127.

[11]Cunningham, *Historical Theology,* 2:342-43.

work of Christ to those who are saved is different from that which it bears to those who are lost.[12]

A twofold substitution is a self-contradiction, for a substitution which does not substitute is not a substitution. Therefore, it must be concluded that definite atonement is a scriptural and logical implication of a recognition of the penal substitutionary nature of the atonement. Christ was either a substitute for all mankind or He was not. If the sins of those who die in unbelief were imputed to Christ as their substitute, why is their destiny eternal punishment? Are not a great multitude of sinners already in hell because of their sins?

If Christ died substitutionally for all mankind, bearing the divine penalty and guilt for the sins of all men without exception, it would appear that at the "great white throne" judgment there will remain no one to be punished, other than the fallen angels, and consequently all men would be saved. "But in fact all men will not be saved, and except for the elect whose sin will be forgiven in view of the work of Christ, men will have to answer to divine justice for their deeds."[13]

Before concluding the discussion of the substitutionary nature of Christ's sacrifice, it is needful to restate Owen's classic argument for particular redemption. It has been over three hundred years since it was penned, and I believe that, to date, no one has been able to refute it scripturally. It is seriously doubted that any shall ever refute it unless the Scripture be rewritten. Owen wrote:

> I may add this dilemma to our Universalists:—God imposed his wrath due unto, and Christ underwent the pains of hell for, either all the sins of all men, or all the sins of some men, or some sins of all men. If the last, some sins of all men, then have all men some sins

---

[12]Roger Nicole, "The Case for Definite Atonement," *Bulletin of the Evangelical Theological Society,* X, no. 4 (1967), 210.

[13]*Ibid.,* 202.

to answer for, and so shall no man be saved? ... If the second, that is it which we affirm, that Christ in their stead and room suffered for all the sins of all the elect in the world. If the first, why are not all freed from the punishment of all their sins? You will say, "Because of their unbelief; they will not believe." But this unbelief, is it a sin, or not? If not, why should they be punished for it? If it be, then Christ underwent the punishment due it, or not. If so, then why must that hinder them more than their other sins for which he died? ... If he did not, then he did not die for all their sins. Let them choose which part they will.[14]

To die for another is, in Scripture, to die in that other's stead that he might go free. To affirm that Christ died for all mankind is the "readiest way to prove that he died for no man."[15]

The priestly intercession of Christ

On earth.—Some modern-day Calvinistic universalists deny Christ's intercession on earth because they do not believe the Bible teaches it to be a part of His priestly ministry. Since they do not stress Christ's death as a priestly sacrifice, the emphasis of Christ's priestly ministry is upon His intercession in heaven—having begun following His resurrection and ascension.

One of the major reasons why the four point Calvinist cannot discuss Christ's sacrifice and intercession as two aspects of His priestly office is because it would necessitate equating the extent of His death with the extent of His intercession. Many who believe this say that, since Christ's intercession commences following His resurrection and ascension, it helps demonstrate that His death and intercession are not co-extensive. Therefore, some divorce Christ's intercession from His death[16] and from the

---

[14]John Owen, *The Death of Death in the Death of Christ* (reprint ed.; London: The Banner of Truth Trust, 1963), 61-62.

[15]*Ibid.*, 178.

[16]Lightner, *The Death Christ Died,* 102. The mere fact that Christ interceded on earth in John 17, regardless of whether it was exercised as a

priestly aspect of His sacrifice and restrict it to a heavenly intercession. The only relationship that exists is that Christ must suffer and die before intercession is possible. Once prove that Christ interceded while on earth as a part of His priestly ministry, and it necessarily follows that His sacrifice and intercession are equal in extent.

Chapters 5 and 7 of Hebrews establish that Christ is an eternal high priest and that in this capacity He is to offer both gifts and a sacrifice for sins (cf. 5:1). The fact that Christ is an eternal high priest should rule out that His intercession could have only been in heaven, for He interceded while on earth (cf. John 17; Heb. 5:7). Was not Christ a Saviour before He ascended into heaven?

The primary aspects of Christ's intercession are His prayers and advocacy, which He offers to the Father for His people. This cannot be scripturally denied. That Christ performed both of these functions while on earth is established in His advocacy for Peter (Luke 22:31, 32), and His "high priestly prayer" in John 17.

Therefore, it is affirmed that: (1) intercession unquestionably pertains to Christ's priestly office and that He exercised this function, in part, while on earth (although the emphasis in the Book of Hebrews, especially Heb. 6:19, 20, lies on His heavenly intercession); (2) the extent of Christ's intercession cannot be separated from the extent of His sacrifice (cf. John 10:10, 15, 26; 17:9); (3) those for whom He interceded on earth are God's elect—both those already saved and those "also which shall believe on me" (John 17:20; cf. vv. 2, 6, 9, 10, 22-24)—these are the transgressors the Messiah is said to intercede for in Isaiah 53:12; (4) this intercession now continues eternally in heaven. More on the latter point follows.

In heaven.—The fact that Christ's intercession in heaven is restricted to God's elect is seen in that the Scripture declares that

---

function of His priestly office, is enough to cause some modified Calvinists to do exegetical "hopscotch" (cf. Lightner, 102-3, 134).

He is able "to save them to the uttermost that come unto God by him [Christ], seeing he ever liveth to make intercession for them" (Heb. 7:25). In an attempt to get around this, some say that Christ performs a twofold intercession in regard to salvation: (1) for all mankind that they may believe; and, (2) for God's elect that they may be saved. In reply to this it may be simply stated; "Why do not all believe?" If Christ died for all mankind and prayed for all mankind that they might believe, why are not all saved? Are not the prayers of Christ always heard by the Father (John 11:42)? Would God have refused prayers for those for whom Christ shed His blood?

Summary

"Consistency demands that the priestly work of Christ be viewed as harmonious and that oblation [sacrifice] and intercession be co-extensive. They are in any case frequently conjoined (Isa. 53:12; Rom. 8:34; 1 John 2:1, 2)."[17] That Christ as a high priest is not the mediator for all mankind needs no proof other than reality. History proves it.

The fact that Christ died as a penal substitute proves that He died only for the elect. The non-elect are justly condemned on account of their sins. To say that Christ substituted for the sins of the non-elect is to say that His substitution was no substitute at all.

The Scripture does not teach an indefinite atonement but a definite atonement. Nicole writes:

> Specially the Scripture represents Christ's work as redemption (Eph. 1:7); Rom. 3:24; I Pet. 1:18, 19; Matt. 20:28; etc.): this implies that the people in view are actually redeemed. The Scripture speaks of propitiation (I John 2:2; 4:10; Rom. 3:24 [25]; Heb. 2:17): this term implies that God is actually appeased and that He does not deal any further in terms of His righteous anger with those who are under the benefit of propitiation. The Scripture speaks of

---

[17]Nicole, "The Case for Definite Atonement," 203.

reconciliation (Col. 1:21, 22; Rom. 5:10; II Cor. 5:18-20; etc.): this term implies that those who were estranged are actually brought back into a relationship of friendship and fellowship. What kind of redemption would this be where the redeemed are still under the power of the enemy? What kind of propitiation, where God still deals in wrath? What kind of reconciliation where estrangement continues to exist and is even sealed for eternity? These three terms, severally and jointly, bear witness to the fact that the Scripture views the work of Christ as bringing about the effectuation of salvation.[18]

Christ in His Resurrection

The relationship of Christ's resurrection
to those for whom He died

The doctrine of definite atonement is further supported by the fact that all those for whom Christ died also died in covenant union with Christ and rose again with Him as their representative head.

> Rising again with Christ is a rising to newness of life after the likeness of Christ's resurrection. To die with Christ is, therefore, to die to sin and to rise with him to the life of new obedience, to live not to ourselves but to him who died for us and rose again.[19]

The express teaching of Scripture is that Christ was "delivered for our offences, and was raised again for [on account of] our justification" (Rom. 4:25). This passage clearly asserts that those for whose offences Christ died, for their justification He rose. If Christ died for all mankind, all must also be justified, or the Lord fails in His aim and design.

It cannot be scripturally denied that those for whom Christ died are those who died to sin in Christ, and they are co-extensive with those for whom He rose. This truth is taught throughout

---

[18]*Ibid.*, 201.

[19]John Murray, *Redemption Accomplished and Applied* (Grand Rapids: Wm. B. Eerdmans Publishing Company, 1961), 70.

Paul's writings. Romans 6:3-11 also answers the unlimited atonement interpretation of II Corinthians 5:14, 15. Both passages undeniably teach that all for whom Christ died also died in Christ. The same truth is also taught in Ephesians 2:4-7 and Colossians 2:10-13; 3:3-4. Indeed, there is no biblical warrant for denying that those for whom Christ died is co-extensive with all those who are saved. Failure to accept this fact is rooted in the failure of universal redemptionists to comprehend the truth of the representative principle of Christ's headship in Romans 5:12-21 (cf. Chapter II).

Summary

As a consequence of Christ's covenant relation with "as many as the Father had given Him," Christ, in His resurrection, rose not as a private person but as a public person, as the head and representative, justifying all those for whom He obeyed and died (Rom. 4:25; 5:18). Concerning these represented ones, Gill writes:

> He has taken possession of heaven in their name, appears in the presence of God for them, and personates them, as the high-priest did the children of Israel, in the holy of holies; and hence they are said to be made to sit together in heavenly places in *Christ Jesus,* Eph. ii.6.[20]

The conclusion is obvious. Those for whom Christ died are those for whom He rose again and "his heavenly saving activity is of equal extent with his once-for-all redemptive accomplishments."[21] There is an indissoluble connection between the death and resurrection of Christ. The benefits accruing from the one can never be severed from those accruing from the other. Only a definite atonement can be consistent with this scriptural truth.

---

[20]John Gill, *Body of Divinity* (reprint ed.; Atlanta: Turner Lassetter, 1965), 229.

[21]Murray, *Redemption*, 71.

CHAPTER IV

PROOF FOR DEFINITE ATONEMENT FROM THE APPLICATORY WORK OF THE HOLY SPIRIT

General

Chapter III has made clear that it is a serious mistake to separate the extent of the Holy Spirit's application of the atonement from the redemptive benefits which Christ procured in His vicarious death. It was demonstrated that to do so in an attempt to make the design of Christ's death unlimited was to sever the unity of the Godhead and, thereby, open the way for one to contribute something to cause his salvation. This contribution, openly asserted by the Arminian, is the exercise of one's free will. Pragmatically taught by the modified Calvinist, it is believing or the exercise of faith in Christ. The former is heresy; the latter is a "first step in the easy descent of error."[1] This initial step toward error does not lie in the fact that faith is a necessary means to salvation; rather, in practice, it makes one's faith the cause which initiates the application of the atonement.[2] As a result, the emphasis in contemporary evangelism has changed from one which actually gives the triune God all the glory to one which acknowledges God as the author of eternal life but, at the same time, makes man's faith to be the initiating or contributing cause of the Holy Spirit's applying the saving benefits of Christ's substitutionary atonement to him.[3]

---

[1]Archibald Alexander Hodge, *The Atonement* (reprint of 1867 ed.; Cherry Hill, New Jersey: Mack Publishing Company, n.d.), 238.

[2]May the reader bear in mind that this chapter in no way denies man's responsibility to believe. The Bible does not teach that man's responsibility to believe is removed because man forfeited his ability to do so through his union and fall in Adam. What is denied is that man's believing has any causative element in bringing about his new birth.

[3]Some contemporary works stressing the grace of God in Evangelism are: Iain Murray, *The Invitation System* (London: The Banner of Truth Trust, 1967); James E. Adams, *Decisional Regeneration* (Allentown, Pennsylvania:

Theologically, this means that faith must precede the new birth (regeneration). Whether this order is understood chronologically or logically makes little difference. The result is that the emphasis in one's salvation ultimately centers upon the act of man's believing and not upon the effectual application of God's free grace.

During the seventeenth century, this theological deviation was systematized into Reformation Christianity through Moyse Amyraut and the School of Saumur in France.[4] This school modified historic Calvinism, especially on the extent of the atonement, and taught that Christ died for each and every individual of mankind upon the condition that each one believe. But, since no one could believe of himself, God elected some to be the recipients of special grace in order to make their salvation sure when they believed. The same teaching is found in writings of the modified Calvinists today. For instance, one writes: "The divine design of the atonement was to provide a basis for salvation for all and to secure it to those who believe."[5]

A lengthy discussion could be undertaken to establish that faith cannot possibly precede regeneration either chronologically or logically and, thereby, make a strong case for definite

---

Sword and Trowel Publishers, 1973); J. I. Packer, Introductory Essay to John Owen's *The Death of Death in the Death of Christ* (added to a reprint from Vol. 10 of Owen's Works, published in 1852 by Johnstone and Hunter, Edinburgh, and ed. by William H. Goold; London: The Banner of Truth Trust, 1959), (first privately printed by Ben K. Howard, M.D., Dallas, Texas); J. I. Packer, *Evangelism and the Sovereignty of God* (Chicago: Inter-Varsity Press, 1961); John Cheeseman, and others, *The Grace of God in the Gospel* (London: The Banner of Truth Trust, 1972).

[4]Cf. Brain G. Armstrong, *Calvinism and the Amyraut Heresy* (Madison, Wisconsin: The University of Wisconsin Press, 1969), xx., 330 (a scholarly work by a sympathetic Amyraldian which would be better entitled: "Amyraut and the Calvinism Heresy").

[5]Robert P. Lightner, *The Death Christ Died—A Case for Unlimited Atonement* (Des Plaines, Illinois: Regular Baptist Press, 1967), 96.

atonement. However, the doctrine of definite atonement can be established without going into detail on the order of the application of the atonement. For this, the reader is directed to the Epistle of I John, which explicitly teaches that the new birth precedes faith[6] and to Murray's work on redemption.[7]

The purpose of this chapter is twofold: to prove that saving faith[8] is in fact a gift of God and to prove that saving faith, which is a gift of God through the regenerating work of the Holy Spirit, demands and is consistent only with the doctrine of definite atonement. Objections concerning saving faith made by both Arminians and modified Calvinists will be answered in the context. The reader should observe that the last centered subheading in this chapter deviates from the preceding format of this work, drawing somewhat extensively from volume ten of John Owen's works (cf. bibliography). This deviation in format concerns the so-called condition of salvation, which man must fulfill to obtain eternal life. Since this condition is said to be faith in Christ and since faith is involved more properly under the application of the atonement by the Spirit of God, this last major subheading is included in this chapter, although the object of faith is Christ and not the Holy Spirit.

---

[6]"Whosoever believeth (present participle active) that Jesus is the Christ is born (perfect indicative passive) of God" (I John 5:1). The perfect tense, as used here, reveals that the one who believes has already been born again— whether this is logical or chronological makes no difference. The point is that regeneration precedes faith, whether understood logically or chronologically or both. The term "born" in this verse strongly supports that it is the inception of salvation that is being emphasized by the Apostle John.

[7]John Murray, *Redemption Accomplished and Applied* (Grand Rapids: Wm. B. Eerdmans Publishing Company, 1955), 79-87.

[8]Cf. the October 1974 issue of "Sword and Trowel" which has two clearly written articles on saving faith by Arthur W. Pink and Charles Haddon Spurgeon.

Saving Faith—a Gift of God

The problem

To admit that saving faith is a gift of God should, biblically and logically, lead one to see that the sacrifice and application of the atonement are co-extensive. All Arminians and those modified Calvinists who reject the doctrine of unconditional election deny that saving faith is a free gift. (Most four point Calvinists who believe in unconditional election hold that saving faith is a gift of God.) The theological controversy over whether or not saving faith is a gift of God appears to stem not only from the doctrine of the extent of the atonement but also from what is meant by the term "justification by faith." The problem, then, reduces to this: "Faith, after all, is something in man; and therefore, if justification depends upon our faith, it depends apparently upon us as well as upon God."[9]

In spite of the fact that most evangelicals admit that faith means receiving something, not doing something, the controversy still exists. Where, then, lies the heart of the problem? It is not to be found in the interpretation of justification by faith but in the interpretation of justification by faith through grace alone. Concerning this problem, it has been well stated that—

> the principle of *sola fide* [solely by faith] is not rightly understood till it is seen as anchored in the broader principle of *sola gratia* [solely by grace]. What is the source and status of faith? Is it the God-given means whereby the God-given justification is received, or is it a condition of justification which it is left to man to fulfil? Is it a part of God's gift of salvation, or is it man's own contribution to salvation? Is our salvation wholly of God, or does it ultimately depend on something that we do for ourselves?[10]

---

[9]J. Gresham Machen, *What Is Faith?* (Grand Rapids: Wm. B. Eerdmans Publishing Company, 1925), 172.

[10]J. I. Packer and O. R. Johnston, "Historical and Theological Introduction" to Martin Luther's *The Bondage of the Will,* trans. by Packer and Johnston (Westwood, New Jersey: Fleming H. Revell Company, 1957), 59.

It is my conviction that salvation by faith, properly understood in the light of the doctrine of free grace, will never provide a basis for one to say that it is his faith which saved him, or that he had any part whatsoever in saving himself. On the contrary, it will cause him to say "God saved me through grace alone." Concerning the centrality of the doctrine of grace in understanding salvation by faith, Machen writes that the "core of the whole Bible is the doctrine of the grace of God—the grace of God which depends not one whit upon anything that is in man."[11] But, if saving faith is not a gift, it certainly opens the door for one ultimately to say that is was "my faith" which saved me. And this opens the door for boasting (Eph. 2:9), because this kind of faith would then make one "to differ from another" (I Cor. 4:7), would it not?

Proof that saving faith is a gift

From the doctrine of total depravity

In Adam, through his first sin, mankind was legally constituted a fallen and condemned race (Rom. 5:18). As a result, Adam lost his freedom of will to do any good to satisfy God.[12] Because of his headship over fallen mankind, each person comes into existence with a will totally adverse to God (Rom. 3:11) and with a total inability to savingly believe in Christ. It is a fact that fallen man must be divinely drawn to Christ; otherwise, he can never come to Christ (John 6:44; cf. Matt. 11:27). Interrogatively stated, the evangelical Arminian may be asked: "How can a lost person who is spiritually dead in trespasses and sins (Eph. 2:1), by his own innate ability (which he does not have, cf. John 6:63),

---

[11]Machen, *What Is Faith?* 173.

[12]The term "will" is commonly misunderstood. In fact, some of the most difficult problems in theology have arisen from a confusion of this term in its relationship to the psychology of the soul. Cf. my "Doctrine of Original Sin in New England Theology: From Jonathan Edwards to Edwards Amasa Park" (unpublished Th.D. dissertation, Dallas Theological Seminary, 1972), 14-20.

correctly understand and interpret spiritual truth (I Cor. 2:14)?"
Likewise the modified Calvinist may be asked: "How can a lost
person savingly believe in Christ when saving faith is a free gift
of God (Jas. 1:18) and when, by nature, man is at enmity with
God (Rom. 5:10) and will not (John 1:13) and cannot (John 6:44)
come to God because he is enslaved to sin (John 8:34), loving
only to practice evil deeds continually (John 3:19)?" The biblical
answer to both of these questions is that man can neither actually
nor logically cause nor contribute any efficacy to his salvation
because he is spiritually unable to do so, that is, totally depraved.
"With man it is impossible, but not with God; for with God all
things are possible" (Mark 10:27). But, if a believer's faith
originates from a free gift of God, then why does not God the
Holy Spirit regenerate each and every individual if God the Son
actually died for them? Is not the will of the blessed trinity one
and undivided? Did not the Son come down from heaven to do
the will of the Father (John 6:38)? Is it the will of the Father to
give eternal life to all mankind without exception because Christ
died for them upon the condition of faith, or is it the will of the
Father to give eternal life to as many as He gave Christ to die for
(John 17:2)? Is an indefinite atonement (whether viewed from an
Arminian or modified Calvinist perspective) or a definite
atonement in harmony with the doctrine of total depravity and the
biblical teaching that saving faith is a gift of God? Which one is
in harmony? Both cannot be.

From the doctrine of election

Believers are those who "were ordained to eternal life" (Acts
13:48), who were "predestinated according to the purpose of him
who worketh all things after the counsel of his own will" (Eph.
1:11). And does not He who works all things also create the
ability to repent and believe the gospel through the miracle of
regenerating grace (John 3:8; I John 5:1)? If not, God's plan is
not all inclusive, especially with regard to the means of applying
salvation, and this would mean that the God of heaven and earth
could not be God, and that He could not do whatsoever His hand

and His counsel predestinated before to be done (Acts 4:28). God forbid! But Paul writes to the Thessalonican believers that he is bound to give thanks to God for them "because God hath from the beginning chosen you to salvation through sanctification of the Spirit and belief of the truth" (II Thess. 2:13).[13]

The election of God is unconditional from man's standpoint and particular in design from God's standpoint. It was designed only for those who "were ordained to eternal life," those chosen "to salvation through sanctification of the Spirit and belief of the truth." Not only were the elect chosen to salvation, but the means to this end were also ordained, that is, "through sanctification of the Spirit and belief of the truth." The surety of God's plan of redemption, that Christ will see of the travail of His soul and be satisfied (Isa. 53:11), lies in the fact that the Father has not only ordained to save an elect and redeemed race in Christ, but He also ordained to set them apart by the Holy Spirit and to grant them the ability to believe through the new birth. If the whole of salvation is a gift of God, the parts of salvation, which include faith, must also be a gift (Eph. 2:8).[14] Election, which is the cause

---

[13]Cf. the excellent sermon on this text preached at the New Park Street Chapel by Charles Haddon Spurgeon in 1855. (This sermon has been reprinted separately by the Sword and Trowel. Cf. Note 8 above.) Spurgeon's biblical exposition of this great text on election should silence the unbiblical, contemporary, Arminian theological interpretations that attempt to explain away the biblical doctrine of unconditional election by way of a universal corporate election in Christ, rather than a particular individual election as well as a corporate election in Christ (e.g., the view of Clark Pinnock, previously a theological professor in Vancouver, British Columbia. Cf. his book review in *Christianity Today*, XIX, No. 9 (1975), 21).

[14]I am well aware of the different views on the feminine gender of "grace" and "faith," and the neuter demonstrative "this" in Ephesians 2:8. Although it is grammatically possible for a neuter demonstrative to refer to a feminine noun, for example, in Philippians 1:29, it is better to interpret "this" in Ephesians 2:8 as referring to the whole of salvation. But, if salvation as a whole is a gift, so must be the parts (i.e., grace, faith, etc.). To say that salvation is a gift, but faith is not, is contradictory, unless salvation is by

of salvation, and faith, which is the means of salvation, are solely by grace, free and unmerited on behalf of those chosen in Christ before the foundation of the world (Eph. 1:4).

The Arminian denies an unconditional election and, therefore, consistently denies that saving faith is a gift of God totally without human merit. The four point Calvinist believes in an unconditional election and most believe that saving faith is a gift of God; yet, he inconsistently asserts that Christ died for all upon the condition of faith.[15] He is inconsistent (whether consciously or subconsciously) because an indefinite atonement or universal redemption has Christ dying for some whom the Father has not chosen and whom the Holy Spirit will not regenerate. Is an indefinite atonement (whether viewed from an Arminian or modified Calvinist perspective) or a definite atonement in harmony with the doctrine of election and the biblical teaching that saving faith is a gift of God? Which one is in harmony? Both cannot be.

From the nature of the effectual call

The effectual call or efficacious grace, as it is often referred to, may be defined—

as the instantaneous work of God empowering the human will and inclining the human heart to faith in Christ. Efficacious grace

---

works. Some four point Calvinists, like Douty, are totally without biblical warrant to assert that faith was not purchased for sinners in the atonement of Christ. (Cf. Norman F. Douty, *The Death of Christ* (Swengel, Pennsylvania: Reiner Publications, 1972), 47-48.) To remove faith as a purchased benefit obtained through the surety of the cross-work of Christ, as Douty does, and make it a sovereign bestowment by God, received through believing (Douty, 47), borders upon the error of the Governmental Theory of the atonement—a theory which rejects the penal satisfaction of God's vindicative or retributive justice by the death of Christ.

[15]Cf. the last major subheading of this chapter: Proof that the Gift of Saving Faith Demands a Definite Atonement.

immediately results in salvation in all cases because it is accomplished by the omnipotence of God.[16]

This quote is significant because it is the theological definition of a four point Calvinist. Observe in this definition that faith is attributed to a divine empowerment. If this definition is theologically accurate (and it is according to both modified and historic Calvinists), does it not make faith a gift wholly from God? Concerning man's responsibility to believe, the same modified Calvinist writer adds: "While in the experience of the individual, faith in Christ is a result of choice and act of the will, it is nevertheless a work of efficacious grace."[17] In answer to the Arminian objection to the doctrine of efficacious grace (i.e., that this doctrine is contrary to all human effort to believe), the same writer replies:

> The fact that we need a work of grace before we can believe should make us recognize all the more the inability of the natural man, and should make men cast themselves on God for the work which He alone can do.[18]

Likewise, concerning the objection that the doctrine of efficacious grace is contrary to human responsibility, the same individual again writes:

> It is argued that if God alone can do it, we cannot be held responsible for unbelief. The Bible, however, does not remove responsibility because of inability. Men are judged because they follow actions natural to a sin nature.[19]

To all the above statements, the historic Calvinist would say a hearty Amen. It is also noteworthy that the last quote above does not make the sin of rejecting Christ the only basis of

---

[16]John F. Walvoord, *The Holy Spirit* (3rd ed.; Findlay, Ohio: Dunham Publishing Company, 1954), 122.

[17]*Ibid.*, 123-24.

[18]*Ibid.*, 126.

[19]*Ibid.*

condemnation as some four point Calvinists say.[20] Is an indefinite atonement (whether viewed from an Arminian or modified Calvinist perspective) or a definite atonement in harmony with the nature of the effectual call and the biblical teaching that saving faith is a gift of God? Which one is in harmony? Both cannot be.

From the nature of the new birth

Concerning the new birth from the analogy of the natural birth, Delitzsch writes that man is—

> conscious to himself of that which is effected, but only as the result of a spiritual work that has transpired in the region of his unconsciousness. ... The creature, in coming into existence, is related to God the Creator as the clay to the potter, ... The creature which God establishes in actual existence is therein absolutely passive. Even to assume only the possibility of a conscious co-operation of the creature would be absurd. The like is the case with the birth from above.[21]

To the same effect, a contemporary four point Calvinist theologian correctly states:

> In the act of regeneration, ... the human will is entirely passive. There is no cooperation possible. The nature of the work of regeneration forbids any possible human assistance. ... It may be concluded, therefore, that no sensation attends the act of new birth, all experience proceeding rather from the accomplished regeneration and springing from the new life as its source.[22]

---

[20]Lightner, *The Death Christ Died*, 46-47, 52.

[21]Franz Delitzsch, *A System of Biblical Psychology,* trans. by Robert Ernest Wallis (2d ed.; rev.; Grand Rapids: Baker Book House, 1966), 402-03.

[22]Walvoord, *The Holy Spirit,* 133-134. "Regeneration is God's act; conversion is ours. Regeneration is the implantation of a gracious principle; conversion is the exercise of that principle. Regeneration is never a matter of direct consciousness to the subject of it; conversion always is such to the agent of it. Regeneration is a single act, complete in itself, and never repeated; conversion, as the beginning of holy living, is the commencement of a series,

Concerning the psychology of faith and in reply to those who say, "Yes, but faith is a conscious act of man," Machen writes: "Even conscious states can be induced in supernatural fashion by the Spirit of God, and such a conscious state is the faith by which a man first accepts Christ as his Saviour from sin."[23]

In John 3:3-7 the Spirit of God is said to be the author of the new birth. According to the above quotes, both four and five point Calvinists agree that, theologically, the new birth itself is a non-experiential act, for man is entirely passive in the matter. Saving faith is that conscious "whole-souled movement of self-commitment to Christ for salvation from sin and its consequences,"[24] and it is always the result or effect of regeneration. How, then, can those four point Calvinists who deny that saving faith is a gift consistently defend their modified Calvinism when they also deny efficacious grace? If they believe that saving faith is a gift of God, how can they consistently hold to universal redemption, especially when they say that "all experience," which would include the conscious state of the believer in exercising faith, proceeds from the non-experiential act of regeneration?[25] Their reply is that the condition of faith permits the atonement to be universal in design but limited in application. Yet, according to one of their most prominent theologians, the effectual call is non-experiential "because it is accomplished by the omnipotence of God," which "immediately results in salvation."[26] Four and five point Calvinists both admit that God's elect are the only objects of His effectual call. But the four point Calvinist either denies in practice or glosses over the

---

constant, endless, and progressive." Archibald Alexander Hodge, *Outlines of Theology* (1879 rev. ed.; London: The Banner of Truth Trust, 1972), 460.

[23]Machen, *What Is Faith?* 198.

[24]Murray, *Redemption*, 107.

[25]Cf. footnote 22 above.

[26]John F. Walvoord, *The Holy Spirit,* 122.

theological necessity and biblical teaching that faith must be and is the result or effect of regeneration. Faith, therefore, cannot be a condition of salvation in the final analysis. It only appears to be a condition from the manward aspect of salvation, especially when viewed from man's unregenerate state. But, when viewed from a biblical and theological perspective, faith is not a condition for man to fulfill because Christ has fulfilled all the conditions in His life and death, and He alone is the surety of salvation for the elect. Therefore, historic Calvinists sometime use or understand the term "condition of faith" in a different sense. They say that—

> the atonement was the *only condition* of pardon and salvation. Faith is represented as an *instrument,* or *means* of uniting us to Christ, instead of a *condition* of our mystical union with the Saviour. By faith we are made members of Christ's body, and so soon as we are thus connected with the Head, we derive spiritual life, and ability to love and act, as the limbs of the human body are moved by means of the nervous energy of the brain. Before the mystical union is formed, the heart cannot palpitate with one emotion of love.[27]

---

[27]Ezra Stiles Ely, *A Contrast Between Calvinism and Hopkinsianism* (New York: S. Whiting and Co., 1811), footnote, p. 179. It is true that the term "condition of faith" can become a semantic debate among Calvinists. For, as Hendriksen points out: "One man may assert, 'Obtaining salvation *is conditioned* on faith.' Another insists with equal firmness, 'Scripture recognizes *no conditions.*' Yet, if only the first disputant would be ready to admit that God supplies what He demands, so that the exercise of faith is ever the result of the divine gift; and if only the second disputant would be willing to grant that (at least in the case of those who have arrived at years of discretion) the exercise of faith is *indispensable* unto salvation, and that it is *man*—not God—who believes, it would soon become clear that the dispute was *a battle of words."* William Hendriksen, *New Testament Commentary: Exposition of the Pastoral Epistles* (Grand Rapids: Baker Book House, 1957), footnote 94, p. 196. Ideally, Hendriksen is right. But, in the case of evangelism, it may be rightly asked: "Is the controversy over this term a mere word battle, or is the truth of biblical evangelism at stake?" The answer can be observed in the evangelistic methods used. In the preaching of four point Calvinists, the often stressed implications—especially at the close of their sermons—are that man can or does contribute something to his own salvation

More will be said concerning the condition of faith under the next major subheading. For the present, however, let it be observed that if the new birth is a quickening from the dead (Eph. 2:1), then faith must be a gift of God issuing forth from the new birth. For no spiritually dead person can spiritually understand the Word of God except he be born again, can he (John 3:3, cf. I Cor. 2:14)? And does not I John 5:1 teach that divine life precedes saving faith?[28] (Cf. footnote 6.) Is an indefinite atonement (whether viewed from an Arminian or modified Calvinist perspective) or a definite atonement in harmony with

---

when he believes (i.e., *he* has met the condition, e.g., "I opened *my* heart," "I decided for Christ," "I let Christ sit upon the throne of *my* heart," etc.). Is this not leaven that, to a varying degree, glorifies man, rather than God? And is not the cause of this leaven, at least in part, attributable to using or misusing the term "condition of faith"? I am convinced that it is. And this style of preaching is not new. Iain Murray has stated that Spurgeon noted with concern in 1890 the new style of exhortations which was being used by preachers and teachers seeking a response from their hearers. Spurgeon declared: "The gospel is, 'Believe on the Lord Jesus Christ, and thou shalt be saved.' If we think we shall do more good by substituting another exhortation for the gospel command, we shall find ourselves landed in serious difficulties. If, for a moment, our improvements seem to produce a larger result than the old gospel, it will be the growth of mushrooms, it may even be the growth of toadstools; but it is not the growth of trees of the Lord." Charles Haddon Spurgeon, *An All-Round Ministry* (reprint of 1900 ed.; 1st Banner of Truth Trust ed.; London: The Banner of Truth Trust, 1960), 376. Iain Murray then adds: "Terminology which Spurgeon mentions, like 'give your heart to Christ,' cannot be used without violating the New Testament gospel." Iain Murray, *The Forgotten Spurgeon* (2nd ed.; London: The Banner of Truth Trust, 1973), 95.

[28]How much time, if any, the new birth precedes believing is not stated in Scripture, for the two cannot be separated. Saving faith always results from regeneration because "regeneration is inseparable from its effects and one of the effects is faith. Without regeneration it is morally and spiritually impossible for a person to believe in Christ, but when a person is regenerated it is morally and spiritually impossible for that person not to believe." John Murray, *Redemption,* 106.

the nature of the new birth and the biblical teaching that saving faith is a gift of God? Which one is in harmony? Both cannot be.

From the nature of faith

The wages of sin is death; but the gift of God is eternal life through Jesus Christ our Lord" (Rom. 6:23). The reception of this gift is "through faith in Jesus Christ our Lord." But if the commitment of faith itself is not also the result of regeneration, then the gift of eternal life cannot be solely by grace, because faith is intrinsic within salvation (Eph. 2:8, cf. Note 14). Therefore, those who say that faith is causative of the new birth—even in the slightest way—and not resultative from the new birth have added something external and foreign to the gift of salvation. They have ultimately reduced faith to a work of man, which is at least the initiating cause of salvation. But this reminds one of Paul's declaration in Romans 11:6 on grace and works; that is, if election (and, thereby, salvation) "be of works, then is it no more grace." The logic is the same.

> The efficacy of faith, then, depends not upon the faith itself, considered as a psychological phenomenon, but upon the object of the faith, namely Christ. Faith is not regarded in the New Testament as itself a meritorious work or a meritorious condition of the soul; but it is regarded as a means which is used by the grace of God: the New Testament never says that a man is saved *on account* of his faith, but always that he is saved *through* his faith or *by means* of his faith; faith is merely the means which the Holy Spirit uses to apply to the individual soul the benefits of Christ's death.[29]

Humanly speaking, it is difficult to understand why those who believe in salvation by grace are so opposed to faith being a divinely wrought means within man when he is born again by the sovereign and efficacious work of the Holy Spirit. If salvation is divinely wrought, it cannot be humanly wrought; and if divine, it is by grace, and if by grace, it is free and unmerited; therefore, it

---

[29]Machen, *What Is Faith?* 180.

must be a gift of God. How an evangelical believer can biblically and logically deny this is most inconsistent. Is an indefinite atonement (whether viewed from an Arminian or modified Calvinist perspective) or a definite atonement in harmony with the nature of faith and the biblical teaching that saving faith is a gift of God? Which one is in harmony? Both cannot be.

From the gift of repentance

If repentance is a gift of God, and Scripture declares it to be, in that God has exalted Christ to be a prince and a Saviour "to give repentance to Israel, and forgiveness of sin" (Acts 5:31), then it logically follows that faith also must be a gift of God. Yet, Aldrich says that an examination of this verse among others yields no proof that repentance as a synonym for faith is a special gift of God. Concerning Acts 5:31 he writes: "If repentance in this verse refers to a special gift for salvation, then all Israel would be saved."[30] But Aldrich, a modified Calvinist, makes two mistakes in his interpretation of this verse. First, he extends "Israel" to mean "all Israel," that is, every Israelite without exception. But the text does not say that Christ is to give repentance to each and every Israelite, and Paul writes elsewhere that "they are not all Israel, which are of Israel" (Rom. 9:6). Second, when Aldrich says repentance in Acts 5:31 is not a special gift of God, he is also saying, whether he is aware of it or not, that forgiveness of sins is not a gift of God. Now I am confident that Aldrich believes that the forgiveness of sins is a gift of God, for only God can forgive sins (Mark 2:7). Therefore, it is concluded that a proper interpretation of Acts 5:31 establishes that biblical repentance is a gift of God.

Granting, then, that repentance is a gift of God, the question may be asked: "Can one have saving faith in Christ without repentance?" Or to phrase it in reverse: "Can one have repentance

---

[30]Roy L. Aldrich, "The Gift of God," *Bibliotheca Sacra,* CXXII (July-September, 1965), 250.

without having saving faith in Christ?" Of course not. They are inseparable. And being inseparable, saving faith must also be a gift; otherwise repentance cannot be a gift. Is this not true? Repentance emphasizes the negative aspect of conversion and faith emphasizes the positive aspect. Both are the fruit of regeneration. They are divinely wrought in the elect as a result of the regenerating work of the Holy Spirit, who applies the saving benefits of Christ's substitutionary death to the child of God. Consequently, repentance and faith are manifested in the elect's life at the moment of his conversion. Is an indefinite atonement (whether viewed from an Arminian or modified Calvinist perspective) or a definite atonement in harmony with the gift of repentance and the biblical teaching that saving faith is a gift of God? Which one is in harmony? Both cannot be.

From other Scripture

In addition to the texts already mentioned above, there are many verses in Scripture which clearly teach that saving faith is a gift of God. Some of the key passages are: (1) "for unto you it is given in the behalf of Christ, not only to believe on him, but also to suffer for his sake" (Phil. 1:29); (2) the believers at Ephesus are said to have "believed through grace" (Acts 18:27); (3) the fact that faith is said to be "imputed" (aorist indicative passive verb) to Abraham in Romans 4:3, 9, 22; (4) John 1:12, 13 and James 1:18 clearly teach that the power to receive Christ comes by the will of God, which means that faith must be a gift of God, for man cannot will of himself to receive (believe, have faith in) Christ; (5) believers know that the Son of God is come because He "hath given us an understanding, that we may know him that is true" (I John 5:20), and to know Christ involves saving faith; yet, the understanding spoken about here is an understanding given to us by Christ; (6) "no man can say that Jesus is the Lord but by the Holy Ghost" (I Cor. 12:2); and, (7) "for by grace are ye saved through faith; and that not of yourselves: it is the gift of God" (Eph. 2:8).[31]

If these key passages of Scripture do not present a dilemma to both the Arminian and modified Calvinist (even the modified Calvinist who believes that saving faith is a gift of God but still insists that Christ's atonement is indefinite), then let them never fail in any endeavor which they might choose to prove, regardless of how theologically difficult it may be. Is an indefinite atonement (whether viewed from an Arminian or modified Calvinist perspective) or a definite atonement in harmony with the analogy of Scripture and the biblical teaching that saving faith is a gift of God? Which one is in harmony? Both cannot be.

Proof that the Gift of Saving Faith
Demands a Definite Atonement

From the unity of the Godhead

In Chapter II it was established that if the Holy Spirit were to impart saving faith to only some of those for whom Christ died, it would cause a disjunction in the unity of the triune God's purpose in the plan of redemption. Scripturally, concerning Christ, it is written:

> (1) "I came down from heaven, not to do mine own will, but the will of him that sent me. And this is the Father's will which hath sent me, that of all which he hath given me I should lose nothing, but should raise it up again at the last day" [John 6:38, 39]; (2) "Thou hast given him power over all flesh, that he should give eternal life to as many as thou hast given him" [John 17:2]; (3) "My Father, which gave them me, is greater than all: and no man is able to pluck them out of my Father's hand" [John 10:29]; (4) "Then said I, Lo, I come (in the volume of the book it is written of me) to do thy will, 0 God" [Heb. 10:7; cf. v. 9].

Concerning the work of the Holy Spirit, Christ says: "When he, the Spirit of truth is come, ... He shall glorify me: for he shall

---

[31]Cf. footnote 14 above.

receive of mine, and shall shew it unto you" (John 16:13, 14; cf. v. 15).

For those who hold to the biblical doctrine of election, the question may be legitimately asked: "How can there be harmony in the purpose and among the members of the Godhead when the Father sent His Son to die for a definite people and the Holy Spirit to apply salvation to that same people; yet, Christ, out of His great philanthropy for mankind, purposed in Himself to die for the sins of each and every individual, foreknowing that a multitude would perish because the Holy Spirit, in obedience to the will of the Father, was not going to apply the substitutionary benefits of His atonement to each and every one of them?" Does an indefinite atonement permit Christ to do "always those things that please him [the Father]"? These two questions cannot be ignored. But what is the answer if Christ died a substitutionary atonement for all mankind without exception?

From the "condition" that men believe

Argument of the four-point Calvinist

Christ's death was a redemption for all mankind to be applied upon the condition that each one individually believes, that is, exercise faith in Christ. Two lines of support are given in defense of this argument.

First, it is said that the sin of unbelief is not a part of Christ's atonement, for it belongs in the area of the application of the atonement.[32] The sin of unbelief is put into a different category, separate from other sins. In support of this argument, one four point Calvinist writes:

> [If the] question is raised of whether Christ bore all the individual's sins except *unbelief* ... it may be replied that the sin of unbelief assumes a specific quality, in that it is man's answer to that which Christ wrought and finished for him when bearing his sins on

[32]Cf. Douty, *The Death of Christ,* 47, and footnote 14 above.

the cross. ... The sin of unbelief, being particular in character, is evidently treated as such in Scriptures.[33]

Second, the sin of unbelief in Christ is said to be, by many four point Calvinists, the only basis for condemnation. Their proof text is John 3:18. Concerning Christ's death in relation to condemnation, one has written that God's purpose in the cross was not only to provide a redemption for the elect but "also to provide a conditional redemption for the non-elect which becomes the basis of God's dealings with them."[34] Another states:

> It would seem unnecessary to point out that men cannot reject what does not even exist, and if Christ did not die for the non-elect, they cannot be condemned for unbelief (cf. John 3:18). Both salvation and condemnation are conditioned on the individual's reaction to one and the same thing, namely, the saving grace of God made possible through the death of Christ.[35]

Answer of the five-point Calvinist

In answer to the sin of unbelief being in a separate category from other sins, the reader is referred to Chapter III and the subheading on penal substitution (cf. quote 14). Furthermore, there is no scriptural support for placing the sin of unbelief into a separate category from other sins. Sin is sin. Although the sin of rejecting Christ is certainly great and is what receives much emphasis in the New Testament, it is by no means the only way in which man can be justly condemned (cf. Rom. 5:12-18). The first of the following four answers deals with the unacceptability of the sin of unbelief in Christ being the only basis for condemnation. The last three answers focus upon the condition of faith that man must fulfill in order to be saved.

---

[33]Lewis Sperry Chafer, *Systematic Theology* (Dallas: Dallas Seminary Press, 1948), 3:198.

[34]Lightner, *The Death Christ Died*, 99.

[35]Chafer, *Systematic Theology*, 3:187.

First, it is apparent that God has not made Jesus Christ known to all mankind without exception to provide them an opportunity to believe on Him. Both Scripture and history testify that in both Old and New Testament times innumerable men, even whole nations, never so much as heard of Messiah. And, is it not impossible for a man to believe in something or someone in which or whom he is totally ignorant?[36] Even more, is it not true that "he that hath seen [the Son] hath seen the Father" (John 14:9)? But, who can know the Father except "the Son, and he to whomsoever the Son will reveal him" (Matt. 11:27)? Therefore, is it honoring to God's wisdom to say that the Father sent the Son to die for all men that they might be saved, but never caused each and every one of them to hear of Christ, although He purposed and declared that unless they do hear of Christ and believe in Him they shall never be saved? Is it honoring to God's goodness to send Christ to die for all mankind, yet never permit, through providence, some of them that perish to learn of Christ, rather to damn them for not believing in Him? Is it not more honoring to God's wisdom to say that all power has been given unto Christ "in heaven and earth" (Matt. 28:18) and "over all flesh, that he should give eternal life to as many as the [Father] hast given the [Son]' (John 17:2)? And is it not true that rejection of the revelation of the eternal power and Godhead in nature is enough for God to justly condemn (Rom. 1:20), apart from the sin of unbelief in Christ? Does not the biblical fact that all mankind sinned in Adam serve as a just basis for God to condemn (cf. Rom. 5:12ff.)? If it be asked why God did not purpose that all

---

[36]Chafer and those who are in theological accord with him should agree with this statement, for as Chafer stated: "It would seem unnecessary to point out that man cannot reject what does not exist." (Cf. quote 34 in the text.) And if a person has never heard of Christ, how can he be guilty of rejecting Him? Then, why does a heathen who dies in unbelief having never heard of Christ go to a Christless eternity? Because of his union with Adam and imputed sin (cf. Rom. 5:14, 18), and rejection of the "eternal power and Godhead," which is revealed through nature (cf. Rom. 1:20).

men should know Messiah, the only biblical reason that can be given is "even so, Father: for so it seemed good in thy sight" (Matt. 11:26).

The second answer is found in the nature of the condition itself. Is the condition for man to believe within the power of man to do of himself? If it is, then do all men have power to believe? To say yes is to deny the teaching of Scripture (cf. John 6:44, 65; 10:26; Eph. 2:1). If the power to believe is not inherent in man, then does the Lord grant to all men the grace to believe or not? If He does, then why do not all men believe? Why are not all saved? Is not God able to accomplish His purpose in sending His Son to die for sinners? Has not the covenant keeping God of Israel declared: "Yea, before the day was I am he; and there is none that can deliver out of my hand: I will work, and who shall let it (Isa. 43:13)?"

The third answer lies in whether or not the condition of faith is procured for believers by the death of Christ. If faith be not procured for believers, then their salvation is not of grace. But this is dishonoring to God and His Holy Scripture.[37] "For unto you it is given in the behalf of Christ, not only to believe on him, but also to suffer for his sake" (Phil. 1:29). Or, if faith be a fruit (gift) of the death of Christ, why is it not given to all men since He died for all men (assuming that He did)? Does not Romans 8:32 state that those for whom Christ was crucified will be freely given all things in Him (cf. Eph. 1:3)? It may be asked: "If a four point Calvinist holding to universal redemption believes that saving faith is a gift of God and that Christ's death was a penal-satisfaction for man's sins (i.e., a satisfaction of the retributive justice of God), then how can he logically escape holding to universal salvation?" Faith is not a work, and the retributive justice of God has been satisfied for those whom Christ died. If they are all mankind, then all must be saved; otherwise Christ has

---

[37]Cf. Douty's position in footnote 14 above.

failed in His design, unless man's sins are punished twice. Is this the teaching of Scripture? God forbid!

The fourth answer to the argument is this: If one must believe to cause his salvation, then this makes Christ only a partial mediator. To say that Christ did not procure the means of salvation as well as its basis and end is to make Christ a partial mediator. The result is that salvation is not totally of the Lord and God does not receive all the glory in saving a lost sinner. But does not the eternal God declare: "I will not give my glory unto another" (Isa. 48:11)?

Two conclusions result from the above answers. First, Christ did not die for any upon condition if they do believe, but He died for all of God's elect that they will believe and believing have eternal life. Second, faith itself is among the principal effects and fruits of the death of Christ. Therefore, salvation is bestowed conditionally only as viewed from a human standpoint. For a lost sinner to experience salvation, he must believe. But one's faith or believing, which is the condition for man, is also absolutely procured by Christ. When this truth is seen by the believer as he grows in the grace and knowledge of Christ, will he not cry out to God: "0 God, why me?"

From the surety of Christ's death

The argument logically stated

If Christ died a substitutionary death for all mankind, that is, purchased and procured eternal redemption for each and every individual of the human race, then, Christ did this either absolutely or upon some condition to be fulfilled by man.

The answer

The answer will be set forth in five paragraphs—four discussion and one conclusion.

If Christ procured eternal redemption for all mankind absolutely, should not everyone, absolutely and without fail, be made actual partakers of eternal redemption? For what could hinder man from experiencing that which God absolutely intended and Christ absolutely purchased for him?

If Christ procured eternal redemption for each and every individual upon some condition to be fulfilled by each one, then Christ either procured the condition for each and every one or He did not. If Christ did procure the condition for all men, that is, that faith should be given to them, then He did it either absolutely or conditionally. If absolutely, then all mankind will be absolutely saved; but this is expressly contrary to the Scripture. However, if the condition is procured upon condition, then the argument comes back to where it started, which is to argue in a circle, is it not?

Now, either all men are able of themselves to fulfill the condition to believe or they are not. If they are, then all men of themselves, by the power of their own free will, are able to believe. But this is also expressly contrary to the Scripture. If they are not able to fulfill the condition to believe of themselves, then when God gave His Son to die for all mankind to procure eternal redemption for them upon condition that they believe, He either purposed to work faith in them by His grace that they might believe or He did not. If He did, why does He not actually perform it, especially since "He is of one mind, and who can turn him?" (Job 23:13). Why do not all men believe? Why do not all men have faith? Does God fail in His purpose? Certainly not! But, if God did not purpose to give faith to all mankind (and surely this point has been proven), then the four point Calvinist's argument would seem to reduce to this: "God gave Christ to die for all men, but upon this condition: that they perform that which of themselves, without Christ, they cannot perform." But this kind of logic supposes that God purposed, on His part, not to accomplish what He sent Christ into the world to accomplish. Is this not self-contradictory? Certainly it is! Is it honoring to God's wisdom to say that He purposed that which He knows shall never be accomplished? Certainly not!

One well might ask this question of the modified Calvinist: "If the condition of faith is not procured by Christ and if men are not able of themselves to believe, although God through Christ purposed to save all men if they believe (because His atonement was unlimited), then how is it that any are saved?" If this question is answered by saying: "God gives faith to some but not to all," then is this not to acknowledge a distinguishing grace in the saving purpose of God? But, if distinguishing grace be their answer, then Christ did not die substitutionally for all mankind without exception; rather He died that some might have faith, but not all, and this is what the historic Calvinist has continually asserted.

Therefore, it is concluded that Christ purchased salvation for men, in the final analysis, not upon the condition that they receive it, but He purchased it so fully and completely that certainly they will receive it. It is true that Christ purchased salvation for those who believe, but the one who believes does so by means of exercising the gift of faith that the Holy Spirit sovereignly wrought in him through the effectual call at regeneration and his resulting conversion. In summary, man's salvation is totally by free grace through faith, "not of works, lest any man should boast" (Eph. 2:9).

CHAPTER V

CONCLUSION

Summary

The doctrine of definite atonement is in harmony with Scripture. If I were asked: "What is the strongest support for definite atonement?" he would unhesitatingly answer, "the eternality and immutability of God's special distinguishing love." For the modified Calvinist who believes in a special distinguishing love, this argument is irrefutable, based upon Romans 8:32 and John 3:16. Their usual reply to this answer is to say that salvation is conditioned upon man's believing. Although this has some validity in a manward sense, Chapter IV proved that the condition of faith itself is absolutely procured by Christ's atonement for God's elect and for them alone. Christ's sacrifice was proven to be inseparable from its application because the unity of the triune God's purpose in the eternal plan of redemption demands it.

One of the strongest logical reasons for holding to a definite atonement resides in the fact that Christ died for us "while we were yet sinners" (Rom. 5:8). When viewed from this standpoint, the issue is simple. Either Christ died as a substitute, a satisfaction, for the guilt and penalty of all mankind without exception or He did not. The proof is manifested in the end result of redemption. Only the elect are saved because Christ died a substitutionary death for them—those chosen "in him before the foundation of the world" (Eph. 1:4). The atonement of Christ, therefore, must be definite not indefinite.

It my judgment, I believe that Chapters II-IV have substantially proved that the doctrine of definite atonement is scriptural.

For the Arminian universalists, there is no human hope that any of the proofs contained in this work will help convince them that their doctrines of free will and a cooperative works salvation are wrong. But, by God's grace, may He see fit to reveal to some, especially among Calvinistic universalists, that the strength of the doctrine of the everlasting covenant and all that it entails (Chapter II), the co-extensiveness of the sacrifice and intercession of Christ (Chapter III), and the proof that saving faith is a gift of God (Chapter IV) provide convincing reasons for asserting that the doctrine of definite atonement is biblical.

Appendixes I-III, in my judgment, have substantially addressed the doctrines of redemption (II Pet. 2:1), propitiation (I John 2:2), and reconciliation (II Cor. 5:19). Also I believe that these three key doctrinal verses provide no theological bases for supporting the doctrine of indefinite atonement when they are fairly examined by consistent principles of biblical interpretation. Other passages that are set forth as biblical proof for unlimited atonement (e.g., I Tim. 2:4, 6; 4:10; Titus 2:11; 11 Pet. 3:9) were not specifically addressed in this work for the simple reason that, if redemption, propitiation, and reconciliation are designed for and applied only to the elect, the atonement of Christ cannot be indefinite or unlimited in design to include the non-elect. For a biblical treatment of these verses and other verses, which are asserted as teaching an indefinite atonement, the reader is referred to volume 10 of John Owen's works and William Hendriksen's New Testament commentary on the Pastoral Epistles (cf. bibliography).

Practical Significance

In Chapter I a work by A. A. Hodge written over 100 years ago was quoted concerning the main objection to Calvinistic universalism—a form of universalism which has widely permeated present day evangelicalism. He stated:

> We do not object to Calvinistic Universalism ... because of any danger with which—when considered as a final position—it

threatens orthodoxy. We distrust it rather because it is not a final position, but is the first step in the easy descent of error.[1]

Arminian Universalism is only an advanced stage in this descent of error. What Hodge has said with reference to Calvinistic Universalism and where its theological descent leads will be substantiated through the extended quotes which follow. Contained within these quotes are some of the major effects which the doctrine of indefinite or unlimited atonement has upon biblical doctrine and evangelism.

In relationship to doctrine

The history of theology affords abundant evidence of the tendency of the doctrine of universal atonement to distort and pervert men's views of the scheme of divine truth, though, of course, this tendency has been realized in very different degrees. There have been some theologians in whose minds the doctrine seemed to lie, without developing itself, to any very perceptible extent, in the production of any other error. With these persons, the doctrine, that Christ died for all men, seems to have been little or nothing more than just the particular form of phraseology in which they embodied the important truth of the warrant and obligation to preach the gospel to every creature—to invite and require men, without distinction or exception, to come to Christ, and to embrace Him, that they might receive pardon, acceptance, and eternal life. In such cases, the error really amounts to little more than a certain inaccuracy of language, accompanied with some indistinctness or confusion of thought. Still it should not be forgotten that all error is dangerous, and that *this* is a point where, as experience shows, error is peculiarly apt to creep in, in subtle and insidious disguises, and to extend its ravages more widely over the field of Christian truth, than even the men who cherish it may, for a time, be themselves aware of. The first and most direct

---

[1]Archibald Alexander Hodge, *The Atonement* (reprint of 1867 ed.; Cherry Hill, New Jersey: Mack Publishing Company, n.d.), p. 238.

tendency of this doctrine is to lead men to dilute and explain away ... the scriptural statements with respect to the true nature and import of the substitution and satisfaction of Christ, and their bearing upon the redemption and reconciliation of sinners. And this introduces serious error into a most fundamental department of Christian truth. There are men, indeed, who, while holding the doctrine of universal atonement, still make a sound profession in regard to the true nature and immediate effects of Christ's death. But this is only because they do not fully comprehend their own principles, and follow them out consistently; and, of course, their tenure even of the truth they hold rests upon a very insecure foundation. But the progress of error in many cases does not stop here. The idea very naturally occurs to men, that, if Christ died for all the human race, then some provision must have been made for bringing within all men's reach, and making accessible to them, the privileges or opportunities which have been thus procured for them. And as a large portion of the human race are, undoubtedly, left in entire ignorance of Christ, and of all that He has done for them, some universalists[2] have been led, not very

---

[2]Moyse Amyraut, the theological father of four point Calvinism and teacher in the French school at Saumur during the seventeenth century, attempted to combine particular election with universal redemption. This gave rise to a scheme where Christ's atonement became totally ineffectual, since it did not secure the salvation of any one. As a result of his teaching, Warfield aptly states that: "The things that we have to choose between, are an atonement of high value, or an atonement of wide extension. The two cannot go together. And this is the real objection of Calvinism to this compromise scheme which presents itself as an improvement on its system: it universalizes the atonement at the cost of its intrinsic value, and Calvinism demands a really substitutive atonement that actually saves. ... The point of insistence in Calvinistic particularism is not that God saves out of the sinful mass of men only one here and there, a few brands snatched from the burning, but that God's method of saving men is to set upon them in his almighty grace, to purchase them to himself by the precious blood of his Son, to visit them in the inmost core of their being by the creative operations of his Spirit, and himself, the Lord God Almighty, to save them." Benjamin B. Warfield, *The Plan of*

unnaturally, to maintain the position, that men may be, and that many have been, saved through Christ, or on the ground of His atonement, who never heard of Him, to whom the gospel was never made known, though Scripture surely teaches—at least in regard to adults—that their salvation is dependent upon their actually attaining to a knowledge of what Christ has done for men, and upon their being enabled to make a right use and application of the knowledge with which they are furnished. It is very easy and natural, however, to advance a step further, and to conclude that since Christ died for all men, He must have intended to remove, and have actually removed, not only some, but all, obstacles to their salvation; so that all, at least, to whom He is made known, must have it wholly in their own power to secure their salvation. And this naturally leads to a denial, or at least a dilution, of the doctrine of man's total depravity, and of the necessity of the special supernatural agency of the Spirit, in order to the production of faith and regeneration; or—what is virtually the same thing—to the maintenance of the doctrine of what is called universal sufficient grace—that is, that all men have sufficient power or ability bestowed upon them to repent and believe, if they will only use it aright.

Calvinistic universalists can, of course, go no further than universal grace in the sense of God's universal love to men, and design to save them, and universal redemption, or Christ dying for all men. The Arminians follow out these views somewhat more fully and consistently, by taking in also universal vocation, or a universal call to men,—addressed to them either through the word, or through the works of creation and providence,—to trust in Christ, or at least in God's offered mercy, accompanied, in every instance, with grace sufficient to enable them to accept of this call. In like manner, it is nothing more than a consistent and natural following out of the universal grace and universal redemption, to deny the

---

Salvation (rev. ed.; Grand Rapids: Wm. B. Eerdmans Publishing Co., 1966), 95-96, 98.

doctrine of election, and thus to overturn the sovereignty of God in the salvation of sinners; and it is not to be wondered at, that some have gone further still, and asserted the doctrine of universal salvation,-the only doctrine that really removes any of the difficulties of this mysterious subject, though, of course, it does so at the expense of overturning the whole authority of revelation. Men have stopped at all these various stages, and none are to be charged with holding anything which they disclaim; but experience, and the nature of the case, make it plain enough, that the maintenance of universal grace and universal atonement has a tendency to lead men in the direction we have indicated; and this consideration should impress upon us the necessity of taking care lest we should incautiously admit views which may, indeed, seem plausible and innocent, but which may eventually involve us in dangerous error.[3]

In relationship to evangelism

Modern Evangelicalism, by and large, has ceased to preach the gospel in the old way, and we frankly admit that the new gospel, in so far as it deviates from the old, seems to us a distortion of the biblical message. And we can now see what has gone wrong. Our theological currency has been debased. Our minds have been conditioned to think of the Cross as a redemption which does less than redeem, and of Christ as a Saviour who does less than save, and of God's love as a weak affection which cannot keep anyone from hell without help, and of faith as the human help which God needs for this purpose. As a result, we are no longer free either to believe the biblical gospel or to preach it. We cannot believe it, because our thoughts are caught in the toils of synergism. We are haunted by the Arminian idea that if faith and unbelief are to be responsible acts, they must be independent acts; hence we are not free to believe that we are saved entirely by divine grace through a faith which is itself God's gift and flows to us from Calvary. Instead, we involve ourselves in a bewildering kind of double-

---

[3]William Cunningham, *Historical Theology* (4th ed.; London: The Banner of Truth Trust, 1960), 2:367-69.

think about salvation, telling ourselves one moment that it all depends on God and [the] next moment that it depends on us. The resultant mental muddle deprives God of much of the glory that we should give Him as author and finisher of salvation, and ourselves of much of the comfort we might draw from knowing that God is for us.

And when we come to preach the gospel, our false preconceptions make us say just the opposite of what we intend. We want (rightly) to proclaim Christ as Saviour; yet we end up saying that Christ, having made salvation possible, has left us to become our own saviours. It comes about in this way. We want to magnify the saving grace of God and the saving power of Christ. So we declare that God's redeeming love extends to every man, and that Christ has died to save every man, and we proclaim that the glory of divine mercy is to be measured by these facts. And then, in order to avoid universalism, we have to depreciate all that we were previously extolling, and to explain that, after all, nothing that God and Christ have done can save us unless we add something to it; the decisive factor which actually saves us is our own believing. What we say comes to this—that Christ saves us with our help; and what that means, when one thinks it out, is this-that we save ourselves with Christ's help. This is a hollow anticlimax. But if we start by affirming that God has a saving love for all, and Christ died a saving death for all, and yet balk at becoming universalists, there is nothing else that we can say. And let us be clear on what we have done when we have put the matter in this fashion. We have not exalted grace and the Cross; we have cheapened them. We have limited the atonement far more drastically than Calvinism does, for whereas Calvinism asserts that Christ's death, as such, saves all whom it was meant to save, we have denied that Christ's death, as such, is sufficient to save any of them. We have flattered impenitent sinners by assuring them that it is in their power to repent and believe, though God cannot make them do it. Perhaps we have also trivialised faith and repentance in order to make this assurance plausible ("it's very simple just open your heart to the Lord ... "). Certainly, we have effectively denied God's sovereignty, and undermined the basic conviction of religion that man is always in

God's hands. In truth, we have lost a great deal. And it is, perhaps, no wonder that our preaching begets so little reverence and humility, and that our professed converts are so self-confident and so deficient in self-knowledge, and in the good works which Scripture regards as the fruit of true repentance.[4]

Concluding Statements

The doctrine of the atonement is of fundamental importance both theologically and practically. The atonement is important because it is, in the person of Christ, a key doctrine of the Christian faith. It is God's means of accomplishing His glorious plan of restoring a redeemed race to communion with the eternal deity. It involves the work of the triune Godhead in saving lost sinners. It is central in the purpose of Christ's earthly ministry as He, the incarnate Son of God, came "to save that which was lost" (Luke 19:10) and to "minister, and to give his life a ransom for many" (Matt. 20:28).

On the other hand, it is dangerous to believe in an atonement which is provisional for all mankind without exception and dependent upon one's faith. It is dangerous regardless of whether or not the emphasis upon the will of man is intentional or unintentional. It is dangerous because the impression is unavoidably given that it is only one's faith which can save him- as though faith were the cause of salvation. In this regard I am in full agreement with Cunningham where he writes:

> With special reference to the peculiar errors of the present time, there are two dangers to be jealously guarded against: first, the danger of attempting to make the cross of Christ more attractive to men,—to make the representations of the scheme of redemption better fitted, as we may fancy, to encourage and persuade men to come to Christ, and to trust in Him, by keeping back, or explaining

---

[4]J. I. Packer, Introductory Essay to John Owen's *The Death of Death in the Death of Christ* (added to a reprint from Vol. 10 of Owen's Works, published in 1852 by Johnstone and Hunter, Edinburgh, and ed. by William H. Goold; London: The Banner of Truth Trust, 1959), 13-15.

away, anything which God has revealed to us regarding it,—by failing to bring out, in its due order and right relations, every part of the scheme of revealed truth; and, secondly, the danger of underrating the value and the efficacy of the shedding of Christ's precious blood, of the decease which He once accomplished at Jerusalem, as if it were fitted and intended merely to remove legal obstacles, and to open a door for salvation to all, and not to effect and secure the actual salvation of an innumerable multitude,—as if it did not contain a certain provision—an effectual security—that Christ should see of the travail of His soul and be satisfied; that He should appear at length before His Father's throne, with the whole company of the ransomed,—with all whom He washed from their sins in His own blood, and made kings and priests unto God, saying, "Behold, I and the children whom Thou hast given Me!"[5]

In brief, I see no purpose, benefit, or comfort in a redemption that does not redeem, a propitiation that does not propitiate, a reconciliation that does not reconcile; neither does he have any faith in a hypothetical salvation for hypothetical believers. Rather, he has faith in a redemption which infallibly secures the salvation of each and everyone for whom it was designed, namely, "the children of God that were scattered abroad" (John 11:52), which is such a multitude of sinners declared righteous that no man can number them. God forbid, therefore, "that I should glory, save in the cross of our Lord Jesus Christ" (Gal. 6:14).

In concluding this study, it is my desire for those who read it that they read and study it through in its entirety. I do not ask or expect that all Calvinists will agree with it, but do ask both the modified Calvinists and evangelical Arminians to understand it objectively and to quote from it contextually. It is also my earnest desire that the reader should understand that the writer's opposition to the doctrine of indefinite atonement is a doctrinal issue and not a personal attack upon those who espouse indefinite

---

[5]Cunningham, *Historical Theology*, 2:370.

atonement. Every born again believer should be ready to have his theological views judged by Scripture without taking personal affront. Therefore, a distinction must be made between the errors propounded by Christians and the Christians themselves. All that are within the circle of Christ's love must be within the circle of the Christian's love. To contend for doctrine in a manner which ignores this truth is a rending of the unity of the true Church which is Christ's body, the elect of God. [6]

---

[6]Cf. lain Murray, *The Forgotten Spurgeon* (2nd ed.; London: The Banner of Truth Trust, 1973), 64-66.

APPENDIX I

REDEMPTION IN II PETER 2:1
(A DOCTRINAL STUDY ON THE EXTENT OF THE
ATONEMENT)

Introduction

In discussing the design or extent of the atonement, there are three key doctrinal terms which are related to the priestly sacrifice of Christ on earth, that is, to the finished work of Christ. These terms are redemption, propitiation and reconciliation. Those who hold that there is a universal design of the atonement which provides salvation for all mankind without exception or which places all of Adam's posterity in a savable state (e.g., both the evangelical Arminians[1] and Calvinistic "four point" universalists or modified Calvinists[2]) contend that there is a twofold application of these three doctrinal terms—an actual application for those who believe, a provisional application for those who die in unbelief. The historic "five point" or consistent

---

[1]Evangelical Arminianism patterned after that of Wesleyan Methodism stresses the truth of justification by faith but holds to universal redemption and a possibility for all mankind to be saved if man will cooperate with God's grace, which was sufficiently restored to mankind after the fall by virtue of Christ's universal atonement. Man, because of the atonement, has the ability to savingly respond to God if he chooses by his own free will.

[2]Calvinistic universalism (modified or four point Calvinism) is that teaching theologically formulated by Moyse Amyraut (d. 1664) of the French School of Saumur. For this reason, this teaching is sometimes referred to as "Amyraldianism" or "Salmurianism." Amyraut taught that it was necessary for God to conditionally will for Christ to die for all mankind without exception in order for God to have a just basis for condemning the non-elect and a just basis for preaching the Gospel to all mankind. This teaching denies the doctrine of limited atonement, the third point of the five points of Calvinism (see the following note) and is commonly held today by many evangelicals. In America it has so permeated Calvinism that, for much of evangelicalism, this form of modified Calvinism is thought to be historic Calvinism. As a result, true historic five point Calvinism is often looked upon with disdain and wrongly charged with being "hyper" and non-evangelistic.

Calvinist[3] asserts that these terms have no substitutionary reference with respect to the non-elect. In contrast to the former, who hold to an indefinite atonement, the consistent Calvinist, who holds to a definite atonement, sees no purpose, benefit or comfort in a redemption that does not redeem, a propitiation that does not propitiate or a reconciliation that does not reconcile, which would be the case if these terms were applicable to the non-elect.

For those who have wrestled with the extent of the atonement, they are acutely aware that there are three key problem verses which the five point Calvinist must scripturally answer if he is to consistently sustain a biblical position before the modified Calvinist that the saving design of the atonement is intended by the triune God only for the elect. These verses are II Peter 2:1, which pertains to redemption; I John 2:2, which pertains to

---

[3]Historic or consistent Calvinism received the theological nickname "five point" Calvinism as a result of its reply at the Synod of Dort in 1619 to a five point manifesto formulated in Holland in 1610 by a group whose teaching later became known as Arminianism, named after its theological father, Jacob Arminius (d. 1609). The Calvinists' response to the five point Arminian manifesto later became well known by the mnemonic: T-U-L-I-P; Total Depravity, Unconditional election, Limited atonement, Irresistible grace and Perseverance of the saints. The third point, limited atonement, is better referred to by the terms "definite" atonement or "particular" redemption because of the negative connotation which it may imply, i.e., that the atonement of Christ is limited in its power or efficacy. What the Calvinist means when he uses the term "limited atonement" is that the atonement of Christ is unlimited in its efficacy but limited in its design to a definite or particular people, i.e., to believers, the elect of God. Historically, five point Calvinism has stemmed from the doctrine of God's sovereignty as set forth in Scripture and theologically formulated and expounded by such individuals and groups as Augustine (d. 430 A.D.), Calvin (d. 1564), many of the Reformers and Puritans, and, in the nineteenth century, the Reformed, Presbyterian and Particular Baptist denominations and fellowships. Within the past few years there has been a revival in historic Calvinistic preaching, teaching and evangelism. Although this revival is small in numbers, it is virtually world-wide in scope, especially in the British Isles and North America.

propitiation; and II Corinthians 5:19, which pertains to reconciliation. If the particular redemptionist can scripturally establish in any of these verses that God's design of the atonement does not extend to the non-elect, then the theological case for the unlimited redemptionists crumples. In summary, if universal redemption in II Peter 2:1 cannot be biblically established, then what purpose does a universal propitiation in I John 2:2 or a universal reconciliation in II Corinthians 5:19 serve? Can it be true that God's wrath is propitiated (satisfied) by virtue of Christ's death for those whom Christ did not actually redeem or has God been reconciled to those whom Christ did not actually redeem? The consistent Calvinist says no.

The purpose of this doctrinal appendix is to set forth a contextual exegesis of II Peter 2:1, the first of the three key problem verses relating to the extent of the atonement. May those who have believed through grace find this appendix of much help in their doctrinal study of the Word of God.

The Greek Words for Redemption

The Greek words in the Bible from which the English translators get the word "redeem" (purchase, buy), when used in a salvation (soteriological) context, always (with II Pet. 2:1 being the only contended exception) mean deliverance from sin by blood, that is, by the payment of a ransom, which is the "precious blood of Christ" (I Pet. 1:19). For example, the Greek word *lutroō* (redeem), in its related verb and noun forms—both simple (*lutron*) and compounded (*antilutron* and *apolutrōsis*)—is used some eighteen times in the New Testament. Fifteen times it is used in a salvation context and reflects the substitutionary nature of Christ's sacrificial offering as a high priest. The price is His blood and the result is deliverance from sin. Three times it is used in a non-salvation context to refer to temporal (physical) deliverance from danger or oppression. In this observation the Calvinistic universalists agree with the historic Calvinists. It is in the word *agorazō* (usually translated "bought") that support is claimed for universal redemption. The prefixed form of *agorazō, exagorazō* (also translated "redeem") is admitted by both four and five point Calvinists to be a term restricted to the elect of God (cf. Gal. 3:13; 4:5). Therefore, the issue on the terms for redemption centers upon the word "to buy" (*agorazō*).

The Greek Word for "Bought" (Agorazō).

The uncompounded verb form "to buy" (*agorazō*) *is* used thirty times in the New Testament. It is used twenty-four times in an obvious non-redemptive context, both literally and metaphorically, with all but two of the twenty-four occurrences referring to such things as a monetary purchase of a field (Matt. 13:44) or food (John 6:5). In addition, it is used five times in a salvation context where the purchase price (i.e., price, blood, lamb) is either stated in the verse or made explicit in the immediate context. In each of these references the context clearly restricts it to believers (cf. I Cor. 6:20; 7:23; Rev. 5:9; 14:3, 4). Finally, it is used once in the well known controversial passage of II Peter 2:1. And strictly speaking (i.e., from the Greek words which have a redemptive connotation), it is upon this verse that the Calvinistic universalist builds his case for universal redemption.

Inconsistency in Modified Calvinism

Before examining II Peter 2:1, it is observed that, in an attempt to prove their case for universal redemption, some modified Calvinists make a distinction between the Greek redemptive words *lutroō* (redeem) and *agorazō* (buy) in their simple and compound forms. But they are not always consistent in holding to their distinctions between the simple and compound forms. For example, one writes that the word forms of *lutroō* (including its compound forms) are "not used of all men indiscriminately but only of believers."[4] He states that the noun

---

[4]Robert P. Lightner, *The Death Christ Died—A Case for Unlimited Atonement* (Des Plaines, Illinois: Regular Baptist Press, 1967), 76.

form *lutron* teaches the releasing or setting free of those for whom it was purchased. He then adds that Paul uses the compound noun form *antilutron* "in relation to Christ's sacrifice for men in I Timothy 2:6"[5] and that it "clearly teaches substitution."[6] These statements a particular redemptionist would have no difficulty in accepting. But when the particular redemptionist says Christ gave "his life a ransom for many" (Mark 10:45), the modified Calvinist is quick to say, "Yes, but Christ also gave himself a ransom for all" (meaning all mankind without exception) and they hasten to I Timothy 2:6 for their support, apparently forgetting that this verse contains the compound noun form *antilutron*. The consistent Calvinist then rightly asks: "Have not all the modified Calvinist's distinctions between the simple and compound forms of *lutroō* (redeem) and *agorazō* (buy) vanished?" For example, two modern Calvinistic universalist theologians[7] list I Timothy 2:6 as one of their scriptural proofs that the extent of the atonement includes all mankind. But, what has happened to their meaning of the compound word for "ransom" (*antilutron*) in I Timothy 2:6? By one's own definition, in another context where the same compound term in this very verse is discussed, it is stated that this word is used "only of believers."[8] But if it is used "only of believers," how can it include all mankind? Is this not a contradiction? (One wonders if such inconsistency results from unguarded statements or if it is the logical result of confusing the contextual teaching of Scripture on the design of the atonement.) To follow their logic would mean a setting free of all mankind, but this is teaching a universal salvation, is it not? Perhaps, then,

---

[5]*Ibid.*

[6]*Ibid.*, 64.

[7]*Ibid.*; and Lewis Sperry Chafer, *Systematic Theology* (Dallas, Texas: Dallas Seminary Press, 1948), 3:204.

[8]Lightner, *The Death Christ Died*, 76.

the word "all" in I Timothy 2:6 is not to be understood as absolute for all mankind without exception. Maybe it should be understood in a relative sense as it is some 500 times elsewhere in Scripture.[9] But is this not what the particular redemptionist has affirmed all along?

II Peter 2:1 and Two Key Words

Turning now to II Peter 2:1, Peter writes:

> There were false prophets also among the people, even as there shall be false teachers among you, who privily shall bring in damnable heresies, even denying the Lord that bought them and bring upon themselves swift destruction.

There are two key words in this verse which have caused great theological debate. The principal one, as previously stated, is *agorazō,* which is translated "bought." The other word is *despotēs,* which is translated "Lord." Almost every universal redemptionist[10] says this verse teaches that the false prophets, who are obviously non-elect, are nevertheless bought (redeemed) by the blood of Christ. Yet they say, since these false prophets continue to deny Christ and never believe, there must be an aspect of redemption (as reflected in this verse by the word *agorazō*) which was designed for the non-elect as well as for the elect. The issue between the modified and five point Calvinists, therefore, is twofold. First, it must be determined whether "Lord" (*despotēs*) refers to God the Father or to God the Son as mediator, or to God the Father or God the Son as sovereign Lord. Second, it must be decided whether "bought" (*agorazō*) *is* to be understood redemptively (referring to salvation or

---

[9]John Owen, *The Death of Death in the Death of Christ* (reprinted from Vol. 10 of Owen's Works, published in 1852 by Johnstone and Hunter, Edinburgh, and ed. by William H. Goold; London: The Banner of Truth Trust, 1959), 232.

[10]Ralph Wardlaw, a nineteenth century four point Calvinist theologian from Scotland, did not hold to this interpretation (cf. the discussion on the Christian charity view and note 15 below).

soteriologically), as most modified Calvinists claim, or non-redemptively, (non-soteriologically), as most consistent Calvinists claim.

Lord (despotēs)

Concerning the first issue in relation to *despotēs*, the following points are observed. First, it is not God the Father who functions as mediator in Scripture; rather it is God the Son. Second, the nearly parallel account to II Peter 2:1 in Jude 4 supports attributing *despotēs* to the Son and not to the Father. Although some grammarians say Jude 4 distinguishes the Father from the Son, the grammatical rule known as the Granville Sharp rule seems to establish that the phrase "our Lord Jesus Christ" is only a further description of the "Lord (*despotēs*) God" in the preceding phrase.

Due primarily to this grammatical support, it seems best to understand *despotēs* in II Peter 2:1 to refer to Christ. Therefore, at this point, it may be stated that *despotēs* in II Peter 2:1 refers to God the Son and not to God the Father. But to say that II Peter 2:1 is speaking of Christ lends absolutely no weight to the modified Calvinist position, for it must be established whether *despotēs* can rightly refer in this verse, or any verse for that matter, to Christ as mediator. This leads to the third point, namely, that *despotēs* is used about thirty times in the whole of Scripture—twenty times in the Greek Septuagint translation of the Old Testament and ten times in the New Testament. But never does it refer to the Father or the Son as mediator unless II Peter 2:1 be the exception. And if this be the case, the burden of proof rests upon those who wish to make it the exception, does it not? Yet, I have not found a modified Calvinist attempting to do this. It is assumed. It is completely ignored that *despotēs* is never used as a redemptive title for anyone, not even of Christ in Jude 4, the only other place where *despotēs* is used of Christ. Rather the dominant use of *despotēs* in both the Old and New Testaments is of God as "absolute sovereign," that is, as "sovereign Lord" and owner of each member of the human race. Luke's account in Acts 4:24 is a clear example of this meaning. There Luke writes of a company of believers who, upon hearing Peter and John's report, "lifted up their voice to God with one accord, and said, Lord (*despotēs*), thou art God, which hast made heaven, and earth, and the sea and all that in them is." Vine's statement that *despotēs* refers to one who has "absolute ownership and uncontrolled power"[11] could find no better support.

Finally, although *despotēs* sometimes has a meaning which expresses the authority that a master has over his servant (cf. Luke 2:29), yet it still does not express a meaning of mediatorship. It is concluded; therefore, that *despotēs* in II Peter 2:1 refers to God the Son as sovereign Lord and not to God the Son as mediator. This does not mean that Christ as mediator is not sovereign; rather it is to acknowledge the fact that when Christ is referred to as mediator, one of His redemptive titles such as "Lamb of God," is always used or the redemptive price is made explicit or stated in the context. But that is not the case here. Search and see.

Bought (agorazō)

The fact that Lord (*despotēs*) refers to Christ as sovereign Lord in II Peter 2:1, however, is not nearly so important, from a theological standpoint, as the usage of the verb "bought" (*agorazō*). Concerning this second Greek word and the issue whether or not *agorazō* is to be understood redemptively or non-redemptively, the following points should be made. First, in the Greek Septuagint *agorazō* and its related noun forms are used some twenty times to translate three Hebrew words (*šābar*, *qānāh*, and *lāqah*), yet it is never used to translate the two great redemptive words—those translated "redeem" (*gāal*) and

---

[11]W. E. Vine, *An Expository Dictionary of New Testament Words* (four vols. in one; London: Oliphants Ltd., 1940), 3:46.

"ransom" or "purchase" (*pādāh*). Second, of its thirty occurrences in the New Testament, *agorazō* is never used in a salvation context (unless II Peter 2:1 is the exception) without the technical term "price" (*timēs*—a technical term for the blood of Christ) or its equivalent being stated or made explicit in the context (cf. I Cor. 6:20; 7:23; Rev. 5:9; 14:3, 4). Third, in each of the latter five references the context clearly restricts the extent of *agorazō* (regardless of what it means) to believers—never to non-believers. Fourth, a word study of *agorazō,* in both the Greek Old and New Testaments, reveals that the word itself does not include a payment price. When it is translated with a meaning "to buy"— whether in a salvation or non-salvation context—a payment price is always stated or made explicit by the context. Fifth, in contexts where no payment price is stated or implied, *agorazō* may often be better translated as "acquire" or obtain." Sixth, *agorazō* is never used in Scripture in a hypothetical sense unless II Peter 2:1 be the exception. Rather it is always used in a context where the buying or acquiring actually takes place.

Four Interpretations of II Peter 2:1

How the words "Lord" (*despotēs*) and "bought" (*agorazō*) specifically relate to II Peter 2:1 may be seen by the ways in which this verse is interpreted. It is interpreted in at least four ways. Two of these four interpretations may be properly categorized under a heading entitled "soteriological interpretations" and two under a heading entitled "non-soteriological interpretations." (See the Chart on page 98)

Two Soteriological Interpretations

The two soteriological interpretations that teach that salvation is in view may be subtitled the "Spiritual redemption view" and the "Christian charity view."

The spiritual redemption view

The spiritual redemption view is held by most modified Calvinists. A proponent of this view writes concerning II Peter 2:1 that "the purchase price of redemption was paid for by the

Lord for even the false prophets and teachers even though they quite obviously never accept it."[12] This view maintains that this verse extends the redemption of Christ to all mankind which includes the non-elect.[13] Hence, Christ's redemption is only potentially or hypothetically designed for the non-elect. That this is a fair statement concerning the Calvinistic universalists is seen in the comment made by the same writer when he states: "It cannot be avoided that Peter is here saying, in words unmistakably clear, Christ paid the ransom price even for those who deny Him."[14] To get away from the hypothetical label, it is often said by those who hold to universal redemption that Christ had to die for the non-elect in order that they might be justly condemned for their sin of unbelief. But is not rejection of the eternal power and Godhead in nature apart from the sin of unbelief in Christ enough for God to justly condemn (Rom. 1:20)? And what about imputed sin, the biblical fact that all mankind sinned in Adam (cf. Rom. 5:12ff.)? Is God unjust to impute the guilt and penalty of Adam's one sin to his posterity? If so, then based upon the same principle, is God unjust to impute the righteousness of Christ to His posterity? God forbid, for otherwise we do not have a substitutionary atonement for the guilt and penalty of our sins and we stand or fall before God on our own individual merit.

Valid objections can be made against the spiritual redemption view by observing what it assumes, teaches and ignores. First, the word "Lord" (*despotēs*) is assumed to refer to Christ as mediator. Yet it has already been demonstrated that *despotēs* in II Peter 2:1 refers to Christ as sovereign Lord. This means that He has absolute power and authority over all His creation including the false teachers because He is their creator. Second, *agorazō* is

---

[12]Lightner, *The Death Christ Died*, 75.

[13]*Ibid.*, 76.

[14]*Ibid.*, 77.

interpreted redemptively to teach a substitutionary payment by the blood of Christ. And since the false teachers are said to be "bought," *agorazō* is assumed to include all the non-elect of all ages. But *agorazō* is never used in a salvation context without a ransom price being mentioned or inferred. And a ransom price is not stated or inferred in the verse or in the context. Third, because of their theological inconsistency, the universal redemptionists do not attempt to explain how II Peter 2:1 can teach that Christ died a substitutionary death for the false teachers, who in verse 12 of the same chapter are described "as natural brute beasts, made to be taken and destroyed" even as they "were before of old ordained to this condemnation" (Jude 4). An explanation of this dilemma is ignored because the universal redemptionist's position presupposes that Christ died for the false teachers. Because of their inconsistency, those who hold to the spiritual redemption view are logically saying, in effect, that: "The Lord, by imparting a knowledge of the gospel and working a professed acknowledgement of it and subjection unto it, separated and delivered from the world certain ones that professed to be saints outwardly, who in reality were wolves and hypocrites ordained to condemnation. Therefore, Christ shed His blood for the redemption and salvation of all the reprobates and damned persons in the world who have lived or will live." Does this make any sense? Does the Bible teach this?

The Christian charity view

The Christian charity view is held by both modified and consistent Calvinists. For example, Wardlaw, a modified Calvinist, writes that II Peter 2:1 "may be easily explained on the principle ... that men are spoken of according to professions, and according to the credibility of the profession, in the estimate of Christian charity."[15] This interpretation is understood to refer to

---

[15]Ralph Wardlaw, *Systematic Theology* (Edinburgh: Adam and Charles Black, 1857), 2:482.

salvation only in the sense of Christian charity, that is, by taking the false teachers at their word.

There is much merit in this view, for verse 1 seems to mean that the false teachers are professing to be what in reality they are not. Furthermore, in verse 1, Peter alludes to the phrase "thy father that hath bought thee," found in Deuteronomy 32:6. And Moses may well be including those in Deuteronomy 32:5 who are not "his (God's) children" within the statements of verse 6 where he says, "0 foolish people" who "do thus requite the Lord." That is, Moses, out of charity for God's covenant love toward His people Israel, may include those who are described in verse 5 as a "perverse and crooked generation" with the meaning that Paul theologically develops in Romans 9:4-6.

> Who are Israelites; to whom pertaineth the adoption, and the glory, and the covenants, and the giving of the law, and the service of God, and the promises; Whose are the fathers, and of whom as concerning the flesh *Christ* came, who is overall, God blessed for ever. Amen. Not as though the word of God hath taken none effect. For *they are not all Israel, which are of Israel* (italics mine).

The major weakness of the Christian charity view is that it does not give proper significance to the biblical meaning of "Lord" (*despotēs*) and "bought" (*agorazō*). This view, as usually understood, takes *despotēs* to mean Christ as mediator and *agorazō* to mean spiritual redemption—both of course out of charity for the profession, not that in reality this redemption is true of the false teachers. This view, therefore, does not take into full account: (1) that *despotēs* should be understood in the sense of sovereign Lord, as a word study supports, that is, in the sense that Paul writes in Romans 9:5, that "Christ ... is over all"; (2) that *agorazō* should be understood in the sense of either God's having *acquired* Israel nationally as a covenant nation as Deuteronomy 32:6b teaches, and as God having made or *created* them nationally as a covenant nation as Deuteronomy 32:6b also teaches (cf. the sovereign creation view below). If this view could establish that *agorazō* was used redemptively in II Peter 2:1 out of Christian charity (and verses 20-22 do lend some credence to this view), it would not support the universal redemptionist's spiritual redemption view because Peter would be speaking out of charity based upon the false teachers' outward profession. Only because of the normal theological usage of *despotēs* and *agorazō* is the sovereign creation view favored (see below).

Two Non-soteriological Interpretations

The two non-soteriological interpretations that teach that salvation is not in view may be subtitled the "temporal deliverance view" and the "sovereign creation view."

The temporal deliverance view

The temporal deliverance view is held by some five point Calvinists. They say that in II Peter 2:1, Peter is speaking of the false teachers, not in respect to the reality of eternal redemption but that, by their professing to be believers because of their "knowledge of the Lord" (v. 20), they are temporally (physically) delivered from the pollutions of the world (v. 20). The Scriptures do, at times, speak of temporal deliverance. For example, the physical deliverance of Israel out of Egyptian bondage by sovereign might (cf. Deut. 7:8; Exod. 15:16). To say that this is analogous to II Peter 2:1 (i.e., that the false teachers escape the pollutions of the world by their outward profession as believers), it must be established that the false teachers in II Peter 2:1 actually profess to be believers both in word and deed. There is good substantiation for saying that they do not. For example, the contexts of II Peter 2:1 and Jude 4-19 reveal that the false teachers actually deny "the only Lord God and our Lord Jesus Christ" (Jude 4) both in word and deed. These two contexts state that the false teachers deny His deity and may infer that they even deny His existence.[16] They deny the "Lord that bought them" by

---

[16]Some object to this view by asserting that the false teachers are only made manifest by their actions and not their words; otherwise it would be difficult to understand how these teachers could gain any hearing with

their actions (II Pet. 2:2) and "speak evil of the things that they understand not" (II Pet. 2:12). They are compared with the ungodly of Noah's day and the inhabitants of the cities of Sodom and Gomorrha, who did not believe or profess to believe God (II Pet. 2:5, 6; cf. Jude 7). In addition they are spots and blemishes (II Pet. 2:13; cf. Deut. 32:5) who follow the way of Balaam (v. 15) and Cain (Jude 11).

The major weakness of this view is that it gives "bought" (*agarazō*), a meaning that is not characteristic or in harmony with its use elsewhere in Scripture. The temporal deliverance view understands "bought" to mean "physical deliverance" from the "pollutions of the world" by virtue of the false teachers' profession (vs. 20). Admittedly, verse 20 does lend some support to this view; therefore, this view and even the Christian Charity view may not be wholly discounted, but the major contextual thrust of II Peter 2 seems to better substantiate that the false teachers not only doctrinally denied "the Lord that bought them," but they also denied Him by their actions (vs. 2) and their speech (vv. 2, 13). They are compared with the ungodly of Noah's day who did not believe or profess to believe God (vv. 5-6; see Jude 7). If the false teachers in II Peter 2:1 professed true Christianity, it would only be in a most outward and hypocritical way. Verse 20 does lend support to this possibility, but in light of the overall context and the usage of the word translated "bought," the following interpretation of II Peter 2:1 is preferred.

---

authority if they denied Christ's deity or His existence, especially in a Christian congregation. However, is it not true that, in many professing congregations, gaining a hearing by denying the deity of Christ is commonplace? For sure the providential existence of false teachers within professing Christendom, in the sense of II Peter 2:1, is only temporary because future judgment upon them is as certain as the fact that judgment fell upon Sodom and Gomorrha.

The sovereign creation view

The sovereign creation view interprets II Peter 2:1 non-redemptively as referring to the creation of the false teachers by Christ their sovereign Lord. There are at least four significant points that support this view. First, this interpretation gives proper significance to both the Greek Old and New Testaments' usage of "Lord" (*despotēs*) and "bought (*agorazō*). Second, this view seeks to interpret this verse in the light of the context, historical background and purpose of the epistle including Peter's use of the Old Testament, especially Deuteronomy 32:5-6.

In II Peter 2:1, Peter intentionally alludes to the phrase "thy father that hath bought thee" in Deuteronomy 32:6.[17] Immediately following the phrase "thy father that hath *bought* thee" are the words "hath he not *made* thee, and *established* thee?" The three Hebrew words translated "bought," "made" and "established" are significant in the sovereign creation view for, in the Hebrew, they mean, in context, "to acquire," "to make" or "to constitute" and "to establish" a nation. The meaning of the Greek Septuagint translation of these three words is "acquire," "make" and "establish" ("create"[18]). Although the Greek word translated "bought" or "acquire" in Deuteronomy 32:6 is *ktaomai* and not *agorazō,* a word study of these two terms reveals that they are closely related and are used interchangeably in both the Old and

---

[17]That Peter is alluding to Deuteronomy 32:6 in II Peter 2:1 may be seen by observing the context of both passages. This is further supported by the fact that Peter alludes to Deuteronomy 32:5 in verse 13. It should be noted that I am not the first to say that Peter alludes to Deuteronomy 32:6 in verse 1, for the same observation has been made by both consistent and inconsistent Calvinistic commentators and Bible teachers.

[18]It is interesting that one of the better Greek manuscripts (Codex Alexandrinus) translates the Hebrew word in this verse for "established" by the Greek word *ktizo,* which means "to create."

New Testaments.[19] A strong case can be established, therefore, from a contextual word study, to substantiate that Peter's allusion to Deuteronomy 32:6 is for the purpose of emphasizing that it is the pre-incarnate Jehovah, the sovereign Lord who owns the covenant nation Israel, because He bought (acquired), made and established them for the purpose of being a covenant and privileged people who were to be unto Him "a kingdom of priests, and an holy nation" (Exod. 19:6). The fact that in Peter's use of Deuteronomy 32:6 he refers only to "bought," the first of the three words in the phrase "bought, make and establish," is explained by the manner in which New Testament writers commonly allude to Old Testament references without directly quoting them. Peter, therefore, only refers to the first word, "bought," using it as a summary for all three words[20] to stress the idea of creating and acquiring Israel as a covenant nation as the context of Deuteronomy 32 teaches. Therefore, the point that Peter seems to be making in referring to Deuteronomy 32:6 in II Peter 2:1 is that just as God had sovereignly acquired Israel out

---

[19]The two words *ktaomai* and *agorazō* are used interchangeably in two Old Testament parallel accounts (compare II Sam. 24:21, 24 with I Chron. 21:24 and II Kings 22:6 with II Chron. 34:11). These two words are also closely related in the New Testament (compare Peter's use of *ktaomai* in Acts 1:18 and 8:20 where *ktaomai is* translated, respectively, *bought* and *buy* in the NIV and *acquired* and *obtained* in the NASB). For a comprehensive word study cf. Appendix I of my "Theological Proof of Definite Atonement" (unpublished Master's Thesis, Dallas Theological Seminary, Dallas, Texas, 1969), 93-101; 108-12.

[20]When a New Testament writer refers to the Old Testament, his use of one word or phrase to summarize the Old Testament context is not uncommon. In addition, those who are not familiar with the New Testament writers' use of the Old Testament should keep in mind that an allusion is just as valid and authoritative as a direct quote, for all Scripture is inspired by God and the Holy Spirit certainly has the right to move the New Testament writers to refer to the Old Testament without quoting it exactly. For example, no orthodox believer would doubt the validity of Rom. 1:17b, which refers to Hab. 2:4. Yet, Paul does not quote Hab. 2:4 word for word.

of Egypt (including 'his children' as well as the 'spot' among them which was 'a perverse and crooked generation,' Deut. 32:5) in order to make her a covenant nation spiritually and nationally because He had created her for this purpose, so Christ, the sovereign Lord, acquired the false teachers (spots and blemishes, II Pet. 2:13) in order to make them professing members of the New Covenant outwardly and individually in the flesh, because He had created them for this purpose (see those who bring heresies into the Church in I Cor. 11:19; cf. Acts 20:29).

Therefore, in reply to the false teachers, Peter might well have repeated the words of the apostle Paul in Romans 9:20-24.

> 20 Nay but, 0 man who art thou that repliest against God? Shall **the thing formed** say to **him that formed it**, Why hast thou **made** me thus? 21 Hath not the potter power over the clay, of the same lump to **make** one vessel unto honour, and another unto dishonour? 22 What if God, willing to shew his wrath, and to make his **power** known, endured with much longsuffering the vessels of wrath **fitted to destruction:** 23 And that he might make known the riches of his glory on the vessels of mercy, which he had **afore prepared** unto glory, 24 Even **us, whom he hath called not of the Jews only, but also of the Gentiles [highlight** mine]?

Third, the sovereign creation view is supported by the context of II Peter 2 and its parallel in Jude 4-19 (cf. II Pet. 2:12; Jude 4). A fourth reason to support the sovereign creation view lies in the fact that it is illogical to say Christ died a substitutionary atonement for those who are ordained unto destruction (cf. II Pet. 2:12; Jude 4; Rom. 9:22). Yet, God in His grace is longsuffering to those who are ordained to destruction (cf. Judas). The definite atonement position alone is consistent with the doctrine of retribution.[21] The identity of the elect and non-elect before the

---

[21]I have yet to find a modified Calvinist who biblically defends his belief in universal redemption from the standpoint of retribution, not even in Douty's work. Cf. Norman F. Douty, *The Death of Christ* (Swengel, Pennsylvania: Reiner Publications, 1972), 120.

salvation of the former is known only to God. And well it should be; otherwise evangelists would not be obedient to God's ordained method of taking the gospel to every creature (cf. Matt. 28:19). But the responsibility to preach a universal gospel does not nullify the truth of God's eternal, immutable, and determinate counsel concerning election and reprobation.

The sovereign creation view thus interprets II Peter 2:1 to mean: "There shall be false teachers among you, who privily shall bring in damnable heresies, even denying the sovereign Lord who created[22] them and bring upon themselves swift destruction."

If there were more textual support for "create" (*ktizō*) in Deuteronomy 32:6 (cf. footnote 18), the sovereign creation view could be more dogmatically acclaimed as the best interpretation of II Peter 2:1. It should be observed, however, that this view is quite close to the Christian charity view, especially when the Christian charity view understands "Lord" (*despotēs*) to mean sovereign Lord and "bought" (*agorazō*) to mean "acquire" as the latter term relates to the acquiring of a covenant people both nationally and spiritually in the sense of Romans 9:5, 6. The Christian charity view understood in this manner properly comes under the non-soteriological heading instead of the soteriological heading and appears, in my judgment, to have considerable merit. Viewed in this manner, it is practically synonymous with the temporal deliverance view. Therefore, it is concluded that any one of these three interpretations could adequately convey Peter's thought in II Peter 2:1. The sovereign creation view is preferred, however, because of the theological and contextual manner in which "Lord" (*despotēs*) and "bought" (*agorazō*) are used in Scripture. But I am not dogmatic in this preference. I am

---

[22]Let those who may automatically reject interpreting *agorazō* in II Peter 2:1, as emphasizing the creative power of the sovereign Lord, make an objective study of how Peter uses Deut. 32:6 and determine why he alludes to it in this particular verse.

dogmatic, however, in stating that *the spiritual redemption view has no consistent theological or contextual support*. And this is the point that this doctrinal appendix has attempted to establish. The reader will have to judge for himself if this has been accomplished.

Conclusion

To conclude this study on the relationship of redemption to the priestly sacrifice of Christ, it should be noted that the Scripture specifically presents Christ's priestly work as accomplishing redemption for a definite people and not a hypothetical redemption which renders all mankind savable. Proof for this is attested by Scripture, such as, "Blessed be the Lord God of Israel; for he hath visited and redeemed his people" (Luke 1:68). Perhaps a better translation would be: "Blessed is the Lord God of Israel; for he has visited and accomplished redemption for his people." (The Greek words *epoiēsen lutrōsin* are properly translated "made" or "accomplished redemption"). This account of Luke's certainly does not teach a hypothetical or potential redemption. It teaches that redemption is an accomplished fact. Luke says: "He *has* visited and He *has* accomplished redemption for his people." Furthermore, can there be anything in God's plan that is hypothetical? Certainly not! His plan is and must be all inclusive, otherwise God would cease to be God, would He not? But His plan is all inclusive, for He works "all things after the counsel of his own will" (Eph. 1:11) and "known unto God are all his works from the beginning of the world" (Acts 15:18). And who can dispute that it is "as many as were ordained to eternal life" who believe (Acts 13:48)?

Finally, it needs to be reiterated that the distinction between the Greek redemptive words and the all-inclusiveness of God's plan does not allow for universal redemption even in a hypothetical sense, such as is claimed by the universal redemptionist for "bought" (*agorazō*) in II Peter 2:1. It is concluded, therefore, that II Peter 2:1 does not teach a redemption for all mankind without exception, and that John Owen, the Puritan, was right when he declared, "'universal,' and 'redemption,' where the greatest part of men perish, are as irreconcilable as 'Roman' and 'Catholic.'"[23]

---

[23]Owen, *The Death of Death in the Death of Christ*, 149.

FOUR INTERPRETATIONS OF II PETER 2:1

"But there were false prophets also among the people, even as there shall be false teachers among you, who privily shall bring in damnable heresies, even denying the Lord (*despotēs*) that bought (*agorazō*) them, and bring upon themselves swift destruction."

	"Lord" (*despotēs*) Refers to	Meaning of *despotēs* in NT When Used of Christ	"Bought" (*agorazō*) Includes	Extent of *agorazō* in NT Salvation Passages	Purchase Price
Soteriological or Hypothetical Redemption Interpretations					
[1] **Spiritual Redemption View**	Christ as mediator	Assumed to be Christ as mediator	Provisional redemption of false teachers	Includes all mankind as the exceptional NT use	Assumed to be Christ's blood
[2] **Christian Charity View**	Christ as mediator	Assumed to be Christ as mediator by profession	False teachers out of charity for their profession; see v. 21	Includes all out of charity who profess Christ	Assumed to be Christ's blood
Non-soteriological or Non-redemption Interpretations					
[3] **Temporal Deliverance View**	Either the Father or Son as deliverer	Not addressed	Either the Father's or Son's physical deliverance of false teachers from the pollutions of the world because of their profession; see v. 20	Includes all who outwardly profess Christ	Not stated in context
[4] **Sovereign Creation View**	Christ as sovereign Lord over all of His creation	The Son like the Father is absolute Lord over heaven and earth; see Acts 4:24	The obtaining or acquiring of false teachers by Christ as their sovereign creator; see v. 13 and Deut. 32:5-6	Only refers to believers; see I Cor.6:20; 7:23; Rev.5:9; 14:3-4	Not stated in con-text. Therefore "bought" in II Peter 2:1 is to be understood in the sense of Deut. 32:6, i.e., "to make," "to acquire," "to obtain," "to create."

[1] Held by Arminians and some Modified Calvinists. " ... the Lord (Christ) who provisionally redeemed them."

[2] Held, with variation, by some Modified and some Historic Calvinists. " ... the Lord who redeemed them according to their profession."

[3] Held by some Historic Calvinists. " ... the Lord who temporally delivered them from the pollutions of the world."

[4] Held by some Historic Calvinists. "False teachers ... shall ... deny the sovereign Lord who made (created) them."

Some Questions to Consider Concerning the Doctrine of Salvation

1. Will or can anyone of himself seek after God (Rom. 3:10-11; I Cor. 2:14)?

2. Does God choose those who believe when they believe, i.e., in time, or before time (Eph. 1:4)? Did God choose (elect) those who believe because He foresaw that they would believe in Jesus Christ of their own will, or because He ordained (appointed) them to believe through the gospel before time began according to the good pleasure of His own will (Acts 13:48; Eph. 1:5-12; II Tim. 1:9)?

3. If Christ died a substitutionary atonement for the guilt and penalty of everyone's sins without exception, how can anyone be condemned to hell for his or her sins (Matt. 1:21; Mark 10:45; Rom. 8:32-34; Gal. 3:13; Rom. 8:1)?

4. Is anyone able to come to Christ by his or her own will (John 6:44)? By whose will is one born again, man's or God's (John 1:12-13; 5:40; 6:64; James 1:18)?

5. If by the death of Christ, God graciously justifies (Rom. 3:24) by faith (Rom. 5:1) those whom He calls according to His eternal purpose (Rom. 8:28; II Tim. 1:9), who can separate them from His love, which is in Christ Jesus their Lord (Rom. 8:33-39)? Who can resist the will of God or ask Him: "Why do You choose certain ones to be saved and purpose to pass by others before they have had an opportunity to do good or evil?" (Dan. 4:35; Isa. 46:9-11; Matt. 11:26; Rom. 9:11, 18-21)

APPENDIX II

PROPITIATION IN I JOHN 2:2
(A DOCTRINAL STUDY ON THE EXTENT OF THE
ATONEMENT)

Introduction

In discussing the design or extent of the atonement, there are three key doctrinal terms which are related to the priestly sacrifice of Christ on earth, that is, to the finished work of Christ. These terms are redemption, propitiation and reconciliation. Evangelical Arminians and Calvinistic "four point" universalists or modified Calvinists[1] hold that there is a universal design of the atonement which provides salvation for all mankind without exception or which places all of Adam's posterity in a savable state. They contend that there is a twofold application of these three doctrinal terms—an actual application for those who believe, a provisional application for those who die in unbelief. The historic "five point" or consistent Calvinist[2] asserts that these terms have no substitutionary reference with respect to the non-elect. In contrast to the former who hold to an indefinite atonement, the consistent Calvinist, who holds to a definite atonement, sees no purpose, benefit or comfort in a redemption that does not redeem, a propitiation that does not propitiate or a reconciliation that does not reconcile, which would be the case if these terms were applicable to the non-elect.

For those who have wrestled with the extent of the atonement, they are acutely aware that there are three problem verses[3] which

---

[1] For a description of Evangelical Arminians and Calvinistic "four point" universalists or modified Calvinists, see footnote 1 to Appendix I above.

[2] See footnote 2 to Appendix I.

[3] Those who are theologically opposed to historic Calvinism should not hasten to the conclusion that the admission of problem verses by the five point Calvinist diminishes his theological proof for definite atonement anymore than the admission of problem verses (and there are many) by the four point Calvinist necessarily diminishes his theological proof for indefinite atonement.

The real issue centers upon what does the Scripture actually teach, a definite or an indefinite atonement? Practically speaking, it is evident that God, in the wisdom of His providence, has not ordained that all true believers should agree upon the extent of the atonement and other important but non-central doctrines. Why He has so ordained is ultimately a mystery to every child of God. We do learn, however, from I Corinthians 11:19 that doctrinal differences in the church are ordained by God "that they which are approved may be made manifest." We also know that, in the wisdom of God's providence, the day of the Lord will come, but not before there is "a falling away first" and the revealing of the "man of sin" (II Thess. 2:3). However, erring on the design of the atonement can ultimately have serious consequences. As A. A. Hodge wrote over one hundred years ago: "We do not object to Calvinistic Universalism ... because of any danger which—when considered as a final position—it threatens orthodoxy. We distrust it rather because it is not a final position, but is the first step in the easy descent of error." Archibald Alexander Hodge, *The Atonement* (reprint of 1867 ed.; Cherry Hill, N. J.: Mack Publishing Co., n.d.), 238. A study of the history of doctrine verifies Hodge's statement (e.g., cf. Spurgeon and the "Down-Grade Controversy" of 1887-92 in England or the theological erosion from Puritanism to Liberalism within 150 years (1750-1900) in New England). For these reasons I am convinced that the doctrine of the extent of the atonement is not to be viewed lightly. Historically, a departure from definite atonement has been inseparably linked with a departure from orthodox teaching on the doctrines of original sin and substitutionary atonement. This, in-turn, has seriously affected biblical evangelism and weakened the Christian's trust and assurance in the one who declares: "I *am* the first, and I *am* the last; and beside me *there is* no God" (Isa. 44:6) and "beside me *there is* no saviour" (Isa. 43:11). I am not so naive, however, as to believe that this series of doctrinal appendixes will persuade any convinced Evangelical Arminian or modified Calvinist that Christ's substitutionary atonement was particular in design for saving the elect only with no saving provision for the non-elect. Such a change in theological conviction only comes from the Holy Spirit and, for reasons ultimately known only to God, He does not in these last days appear to be changing the convictions of large numbers of traditional evangelical Christians whose existential minds are apparently closed, not being in submission to the teaching of the whole counsel of God, especially with reference to His sovereignty and the particularistic design of the atonement. I do believe, however, that these doctrinal appendixes may help many of those who have believed through grace and are open to learning more about the doctrines of grace.

the five point Calvinist must scripturally answer if he is to consistently sustain a biblical position before the modified Calvinist that the saving design of the atonement is intended by the triune God only for the elect. These verses are II Peter 2:1, which pertains to redemption; I John 2:2, which pertains to propitiation; and II Corinthians 5:19, which pertains to reconciliation. If the particular redemptionist can scripturally establish in any of these verses that God's design of the atonement does not extend to the non-elect, then the theological case for the unlimited redemptionist crumples. In summary, if universal propitiation in I John 2:2 cannot be biblically established, then what purpose does a universal redemption in II Peter 2:1 or a universal reconciliation in II Corinthians 5:19 serve? Can it be true that God the Son redeemed the non-elect for whom God the Father's wrath will never be propitiated (satisfied or appeased) by virtue of Christ's death or that God the Father has been reconciled by virtue of Christ's death to the non-elect upon whom His condemning wrath eternally abides (John 3:36)?

The purpose of this doctrinal appendix is to approach theologically I John 2:2, which relates to propitiation—the second of the three major doctrinal terms. May those who have believed through grace find this appendix of much help in their doctrinal study of the Word of God.

Propitiation in the New Testament

The term "propitiation" (*hilasmos*) means "satisfaction," "appeasement." Theologically, propitiation means that God's wrath against sin, demanded by His justice, is appeased on account of the death of Christ for sinners.

There are four primary references in the New Testament where the word "propitiation" is used (cf. Rom. 3:25; Heb. 2:17; I John 2:2; 4:10). Three of the four references clearly teach that propitiation is strictly limited to a definite people, namely, the elect of God.

Romans 3:25 states that God set forth Christ to be "a propitiation through faith in his blood." From this reference it may be observed that, if Christ is a propitiation "through faith,"[4] He cannot be a propitiation to those who never have faith, and "all men have not faith" (II Thess. 3:2).

Hebrews 2:17 states that Christ was made a "merciful and faithful high priest in things pertaining to God, to make reconciliation [should be translated *propitiation*] for the sins of the people." In context, "the people," are identified as the "children which God hath given" Christ, (v. 13), "the seed of Abraham" (v. 16). Are not "the people" of verse 17 also to be identified with the "many sons" in verse 10 and the "every man" in verse 9 for whom "by the grace of God he should taste death"?

I John 4:10 reveals the motivating cause of propitiation. "Herein is love, not that we loved God, but that he loved us, and sent his Son to be the propitiation for our sins."[5] The propitiation is restricted here to the definite pronouns, "we," "us," and "our"; that is, to believers, God's elect. Therefore, it is concluded that at

---

[4]The words "through faith" are grammatically more naturally connected with "propitiation" rather than with "being justified," "set forth" or "through his blood." Hence, it is Christ Jesus whom God has set forth as a propitiation to be received by faith through his blood.

[5]Observe also that the love manifested in I John 4:10 is the special love of God, which is the highest form of His love expressed toward man. It is this special redemptive love, the giving of Christ as a sacrifice, which is the motivating cause of giving all the other gifts of saving grace, the "all things" of Romans 8:32. The immediate context in Romans 8 teaches, among other things, that predestination, calling, justification and glorification are included in the "all things" of verse 32, that is, for all the Christians at Rome and, by extension, for all true believers. Now, if this be true (and it is according to context), is not saving faith also included in the "all things"? Is one justified by any other means than faith? No, not according to Scripture. Therefore, if justification is included as one of the gifts of saving grace in the "all things," then saving faith must also be included. Clearly, this passage in Romans 8 limits the extent of Christ's substitutionary death to God's elect.

least three of the four major passages on propitiation are restricted in design to God's elect.

I John 2:2

Concerning I John 2:2, Calvinistic universalists say it teaches two aspects of propitiation. One writes:

> There is a propitiation which affects God in His relation to the *kosmos*—with no reference to the elect—and one which affects His relation to the elect. This twofold propitiation is set forth in I John 2:2.[6]

The sum of the four point Calvinist position is that Christ is said, in some sense, to be the propitiation for the sins of the whole world, meaning all mankind without exception. This, according to another Calvinistic universalist, is "the normal unbiased approach to this text."[7]

The meaning and nature of propitiation is not a matter of disagreement between four and five point Calvinists. The issue lies in the extent of propitiation as taught in I John 2:2. Much has been written concerning both sides of the issue. An examination of these writings reveals that the crux of the difference hinges upon the term "whole world." The four point Calvinists say the meaning is obvious. The words themselves, they say, without any wresting, signify all men in the world, that is, world means *world*. John Owen, the Puritan, writes, concerning the dogmatism with which all universal redemptionists assert their "darling"[8] proof for unlimited atonement, by saying:

---

[6]Lewis Sperry Chafer, *Systematic Theology* (Dallas, Texas: Dallas Seminary Press, 1948), 3:95-96.

[7]Robert P. Lightner, *The Death Christ Died—A Case for Unlimited Atonement* (Des Plaines, Illinois: Regular Baptist Press, 1967), 81.

[8]John Owen, *The Death of Death in the Death of Christ* (reprinted from Vol. 10 of Owen's Works, published in 1852 by Johnstone and Hunter, Edinburgh, and ed. by William H. Goold; London: The Banner of Truth Trust, 1959), 191.

The world, the whole world, all, all men!—who can oppose it? Call them [the universalist redemptionists] to the context in the several places where the words are; appeal to rules of interpretation; mind them of the circumstances and scope of the place, the sense of the same words in other places; ... [and] they ... cry out, the *bare word*, the letter is theirs: "Away with the gloss and interpretation; give us leave to believe what the word expressly saith."[9]

Biblical Universal Terminology

That I John 2:2 contains universal language is evident from the term "whole world." John 3:16 also uses the universal term "world" in the same manner. It is clear, therefore, that there is a biblical or divine universalism taught in Scripture. However, the issue does not center on the fact that universal terminology is used. It centers on the meaning or interpretation of that terminology.

Four Interpretations of the Term "Whole World"

The major views which are universalistic in their interpretation of "whole world" in I John 2:2 will be discussed under the following four systematic headings: "generical," "geographical," "eschatological," and "ethnological." (See the Chart on page 119)

The generical interpretation

The generical interpretation of I John 2:2 is held by those who believe that Christ's atonement was unlimited in design for the whole human race. Their usual interpretation of the text is that Christ "is the propitiation for our sins (meaning believers), and not for ours only, but also for the sins of the whole world (including the non-elect)." This view interprets "whole world" to mean all men generically or universally, that is, each and every member of Adam's race. Therefore, propitiation for the sins of the world does not save the world; rather it only "secures the

---

[9] *Ibid.*

possibility of salvation."[10] Furthermore, this view distinguishes between the advocacy and propitiatory work of Christ in I John 2:1-2 and associates actual salvation only with Christ's advocacy. This means that Christ's propitiation on earth was and is universal for all men—both the elect and non-elect alike. His advocacy in heaven, however, is restricted for those only who believe in Him. The contingency· of one's salvation, therefore, rests upon man and the so-called "condition of faith."[11] In other words, what now brings unbelievers into condemnation is not their sins—God has been satisfied for them by the blood of Christ—but the sin of rejecting Christ as the divinely appointed mediator of salvation. But Warfield rightly objects to this by saying:

> Is not the rejection of Jesus as our propitiation a sin? And if it is a sin, is it not like other sins, covered by the death of Christ? If this great sin is excepted from the expiatory [effectual covering] of Christ's blood, why did not John tell us so, instead of declaring without qualification that Jesus Christ is the propitiation for our sins, and not for ours only but for the whole world? And surely it would be very odd if the sin of rejection of the Redeemer were the only condemning sin, in a world the vast majority of the dwellers in which have never heard of this Redeemer, and nevertheless perish.

---

[10]Chafer, *Systematic Theology*, 5:197.

[11]Historic Calvinists use the theological term "condition of faith" in a different sense than that of Calvinistic universalists; that is, Christ did not die for any upon condition, *if they do believe,* but He died for all God's elect *that they will believe* and believing have eternal life. Because saving faith itself is among the principal effects and fruits of the death of Christ (see footnote 5 above), salvation is bestowed conditionally only as viewed by the lost sinner. For him to experience salvation, he must believe; but saving faith, which is the condition for man, is also absolutely procured by Christ. Otherwise, if faith is not procured for believers, then their salvation is not all of grace. Where the believer grows in grace and sees that the condition of faith has been procured by Christ, then should he not cry out "0 Lord, why me?"

On what ground do they perish, all their sins having been expiated?[12]

There are a number of observations that can be made in objection to the generical or universal interpretation of I John 2:2. Some of the more significant ones immediately follow; others will be mentioned in the discussion under the geographical, eschatological and ethnological subheadings.

Terminological objection.—The first observation made in objection to the generical view concerns the use of the term "world" (*kosmos*) in the New Testament. That *kosmos* can and does have more than the meaning of all mankind generically cannot be denied (cf. John 1:10, 11; 3:17; 12:31; 17:6, 9, 11, 18, 21, 23-24).[13] In fact *kosmos,* as effectually demonstrated in Owen's work,[14] has many uses and meanings—the usual meaning being "many of mankind."

According to the New Testament Greek text, *kosmos* occurs about 185 times. It is used some 105 times by the Apostle John, 47 times by Paul and 33 times by other writers. With the use of a concordance, it is readily observed that *kosmos* is never used by Paul or the other writers to mean all mankind generically in a salvation context unless John's usage is the exception. It is used

---

[12]John E. Meeter (ed.), *Selected Shorter Writings of Benjamin B. Warfield* (Nutley, New Jersey: Presbyterian and Reformed Publishing Company, 1970-73), 1:172.

[13]Those who hold to universal propitiation in a generical sense are exhorted to refer to Owen's work (pp. 189-95; 204-26) where he deals exhaustively with the terms "world," "whole world" and their equivalents. His arguments for definite atonement in response to the generical interpretation of such passages as John 3:16 and I John 2:2 are irrefutably stated and, in my opinion, can never be biblically disavowed because Owen's arguments are biblical.

[14]*Ibid.*, 191-93. The reader is also referred to Hendriksen's work for a study of John's use of the term "world." Cf. William Hendriksen, *A Commentary on the Gospel of John* (two vols. in one; London: The Banner of Truth Trust, 1954), 1:79.

of all mankind universally in a context of sin and judgment (Rom. 3:6, 19; 5:12), but never in a salvation context.

In John's writings, *kosmos* is used a total of 78 times in his gospel, 23 times in I John and 4 times in II John and Revelation. A check of each of these references, in context, reveals that there are perhaps, at the most, eleven occurrences in ten verses which could possibly, even according to Arminianism, mean all mankind generically in a salvation context. These occurrences are found in John 1:29; 3:16; two times in 3:17; once each in John 4:42; 6:33, 51; 12:47; 16:8 and once each in I John 2:2 and 4:14.

Concerning the possible usage of *kosmos* to mean all mankind without exception in the redemptive context of I John 2:2, let the reader observe that *kosmos* is used differently at least 21 out of 23 times elsewhere in the epistle. As a matter of fact, the identical term "whole world" is used in I John 5:19 where it cannot possibly mean all mankind absolutely. John writes: "we know that we are of God, and the whole world lieth in wickedness [in the wicked one]." Can this be true of the believer who is in Christ? Let the reader judge. If the term "whole world" in I John 2:2 means all mankind generically, it is an exceptional usage in the epistle (objectively, only in I John 2:2 and 4:14 could it possibly refer to all mankind without exception—two times out of 23 occurrences). Therefore, it is my contention that the burden of proof rests upon those who interpret "whole world" generically to establish that the term means all mankind in any redemptive context, let alone I John 2:2. In my research I have not found any writer who holds to an indefinite atonement attempting to do this; rather the term is always said to mean, in a "normal and unbiased approach," the whole world, meaning all mankind,[15] both the elect and the non-elect.

Logical objection.—The second observation made in objection to the generical view is logical and relates to the design

---

[15]Lightner, *The Death Christ' Died*, 81.

of propitiation from the standpoint of the special and distinguishing love of God. The fact that Christ's blood was an appeasement of God's wrath, in order that the chief purpose of God's love might be manifested, demands Christ's death. But if God's giving His Son is a manifesting of His special distinguishing love (and it is), and if "He spared not his own Son, but delivered him up for us all, how shall he not with him also freely give us all things" (Rom. 8:32)? The answer to this question should be obvious. The term "whole world" cannot refer to all mankind generically in a salvation context, for the non-elect do not receive all or any of the gifts of saving grace which (according to Rom. 8:32) is assured to them if, in reality, Christ actually died for them. Do all men have faith (II Thess. 3:2)?[16]

Contextual objection.—A third observation made in objection to the generical view lies in the fact that the context of I John 2:2 teaches that Christ's advocacy and propitiation are the same in design and extent. This is supported by the coordinating conjunction "and," which connects verse 2 with verse 1. Certainly no Calvinistic universalist is willing to admit that Christ's advocacy actually extends to the non-elect. How, then, can propitiation be absolutely universal if Christ's advocacy is not? In an attempt to explain this objection, those who hold to the generical interpretation intimate that it is Christ's advocacy in heaven which particularizes His propitiation on earth and makes it efficacious before the Father. They say that—

> propitiation is conceived as merely laying a basis for actual forgiveness of sins, and is spoken of therefore rather as "sufficient" than efficacious—becoming efficacious only through the act of faith on the part of the believer, by which he secures Christ as his Advocate.[17]

---

[16]See footnote 5 above.

[17]Meeter (ed.), *Selected Shorter Writings*, 1:173.

But this attempted explanation empties the conception of propitiation from its biblical meaning and shifts the saving operation of Christ from His atoning death on earth to His intercession in heaven. However, as Warfield points out,

> no support is given this elaborate construction by John; and our present passage is enough to shatter the foundation on which it is built. ... The "advocacy" of our Lord is indeed based here on his propitiation. But it is based on it not as if it bore merely an accidental relation to it, ... but as its natural and indeed necessary issue. John introduces the declaration that Christ is—not "was," the propitiation is as continuous in its effect as the advocacy—our propitiation, in order to support his reference of sinning Christians to Christ as their Advocate with the Father, and to give them confidence in the efficacy of his advocacy. The efficacy of the advocacy rests on that of the propitiation, not the efficacy of the propitiation on that of the advocacy. It was in the propitiatory death of Christ that John finds Christ's saving work: the advocacy is only its continuation—its unceasing presentation in heaven. The propitiation accordingly not merely lays a foundation for a saving operation, to follow or not follow as circumstances may determine. It itself saves. And this saving work is common to Christians and "the whole world." By it the sins of the one as of the other are expiated. ... They no longer exist for God—and are not they blessed whose iniquities are forgiven, and whose sins are covered, to whom the Lord will not reckon sin?[18]

Grammatical objection.—The fourth observation made in objection to the generical view is grammatical. One contemporary Calvinistic universalist attempts to explain Christ's suffering for the sins of both the elect and non-elect by saying that His suffering was retroactive to Adam's fall and *potentially* available (a better term would be *hypothetically* available) for the

---

[18]*Ibid.*, 173-74.

non-elect both before and after the cross.[19] He explains I John 2:2 by saying that Christ—

> 'is the propitiation for our sins,' which means He is the *actual* propitiation for [believers' sins through faith]. ... But we are also told that He is the propitiation 'for the sins of the whole world,' ... [which] means that He is the *potential* propitiation only [for the non-elect]; otherwise the Apostle would have been teaching universalism.[20]

Is this not an example of exegetical hopscotch by a Calvinistic hypothetical universalist? But what does I John 2:2 actually say? It says that Christ "is (*estin*) the propitiation for our sins: and not for ours only, but also for the sins of the whole world." *The text does not say* that Christ is *potentially* the propitiation for "our sins" and "the sins of the whole world."[21]

Biblical objection.—The fifth and final observation made in objection to the generical view concerns the use of the term "propitiation" in Romans 3:25, Hebrews 2:17 and I John 4:10. In each of these references, propitiation is restricted to believers, that is, to God's elect. Furthermore, when dealing with a problem text, the principle of interpretation which requires one to compare the usage of a word or term as it is used elsewhere must not be ignored or slighted, especially when it is used elsewhere by the same author. Yet this is done by those who hold to generic

---

[19]Norman F. Douty, *The Death Christ Died* (Swengel, Pennsylvania: Reiner Publications, 1972), 29.

[20]*Ibid.*, 32-33.

[21]The verb "is" (*estin*) is in the present tense and indicative mood (the mood of certainty or reality) and governs both clauses in the verse. If Christ is the potential propitiation for the non-elect, why was not the subjunctive mood used (the mood of mild contingency or potentiality which often assumes unreality depending, of course, on the context)? Why does not *contextual exegesis* support the translation that Christ is the *potential* propitiation of our sins and the sins of the whole world? Douty simply does not address this grammatical problem and provides absolutely no exegetical support for asserting that Christ is the *potential* propitiation for those who die in unbelief.

universalism. Why? Because they do not mention the extent of propitiation in its other occurrences when they discuss the extent in I John 2:2. Both the modified and consistent Calvinists admit that there is some ambiguity in the interpretation of I John 2:2; otherwise there would not be the great theological controversy between them over the meaning of this verse. Is it not proper, then, for I John 4:10 also to be considered to determine if it will help remove some of the ambiguity? Does I John 4:10 help do this? "Herein is love, not that we loved God, but that he loved us, and sent his Son to be the propitiation for our sins." May the reader decide if this verse is helpful in understanding the extent of the atonement in general and the extent of propitiation in I John 2:2 in particular.

The geographical interpretation

The second explanation of the universal terminology in I John 2:2 is that termed under the heading of "geographical universalism." This view interprets "and he is the propitiation for our sins" as referring to the recipients of John's epistle, that is, those believers living in Asia Minor. It interprets the latter part of the verse "and not for ours only, but also for the sins of the whole world" to refer to those Christians everywhere outside Asia Minor who confess their sins to Christ their advocate. This view is close to that of Augustine, Calvin and Beza—

> who understand by 'the whole world' 'the churches of the elect dispersed through the whole world'; and by the declaration that Jesus Christ is 'a propitiation for the whole world,' that in his blood all the sins of all believers throughout the world are expiated.[22]

While the geographical view has much scriptural merit and is certainly in harmony with reality, it seems that the term "whole world" conveys something beyond "the world of believers outside Asia Minor." In other words, it seems to be more than

---

[22]Meeter (ed.), *Selected Shorter Writings*, 1:170.

just a geographical distinction. In my judgment this something else is explained by the following two interpretations.

The eschatological interpretation

The third interpretation of the universal terminology in I John 2:2 is that view termed "eschatological universalism," the future world that is saved at the second coming of Christ, which will include all the elect from all ages. This is the view set forth by Warfield and has much to commend it. In John 1:29, 3:17 and 12:47, John declares that the mission of the Son in coming into the world is not only to save individuals but to save the world itself. "Behold the Lamb of God, which taketh away the sin of the world." This, however, will not come to pass until the eschatological future, at the end time, when God's redemptive plan is complete. Then, and then only, will there be a saved world. Concerning this view, Warfield writes:

> It is the great conception which John is reflecting in the phrase, "he is the propitiation for our sins, and not for ours only but for the whole world." This must not be diluted into the notion that he came to offer salvation to the world, or to do his part toward the salvation of the world, or to lay such a basis for salvation that it is the world's fault if it is not saved. John's thinking does not run on such lines; and what he actually says is something very different, namely that Jesus Christ is a propitiation for the whole world, that he has expiated the whole world's sins. He came into the world because of love of the world, in order that he might save the world, and he actually saves the world. Where the expositors have gone astray is in not perceiving that this salvation of the world was not conceived by John—any more than the salvation of the individual—as accomplishing itself all at once. Jesus came to save the world, and the world will through him be saved; at the end of the day he will have a saved world to present to his father. John's mind is running forward to the completion of his saving work; and he is speaking of his Lord from the point of view of this completed work. From that point of view he is the Savior of the world. ... He proclaims Jesus the Savior of the world and declares him a propitiation for the whole world. He is a universalist; he teaches the salvation of the whole

world. But he is not an "each and every" universalist: he is an "eschatological" universalist.[23]

In Warfield's exposition[24] of the term "world" in I John 2:2, he discusses his eschatological universalism view and what I have systematically termed under "generical" and "geographical" universalism. However, he does not mention or discuss the fourth and following interpretation, namely, that termed "ethnological universalism." Although, in my judgment, Warfield's eschatological universalism may adequately explain John 1:29, 3:17 and 12:47 (there will be a future world in which all the sins of that world will be taken away), it does not seem, as presented by Warfield, to fully account for the contextual meaning of *kosmos* in John 3:16 or in I John 2:2.

The ethnological interpretation

The ethnological interpretation asserts that the term "world" in both I John 2:2 and John 3:16, although including the geographical and eschatological views, also stresses that some without distinction, not all without exception, out of the Gentiles as well as out of the Jews (Rom. 9:24) have had their sins propitiated by the death of Christ. It is as though the Lord were saying. "The Jews, Nicodemus, no longer have a national monopoly on the salvation of Jehovah. Do you not, Nicodemus, remember the words of the prophet Isaiah who said, 'I will also give the Holy One of Israel for a light to the Gentiles, that thou mayest be my salvation unto the end of the earth' (Isa. 49:6)? Nicodemus, did not the psalmist prophesy of me when he said, 'therefore will I give thanks unto thee, 0 Lord, among the heathen, and sing praises unto thy name' (Ps. 18:49)?" Did not "the apostles and brethren that were in Judea," when "they heard that the Gentiles had also received the word of God," declare: "then hath God also to the Gentiles granted repentance unto life"

---

[23]*Ibid.*, 176-77.

[24]*Ibid.*, 169-77.

(Acts 11:18)? Is not the term "world" used of the Gentiles by the apostle Paul in Romans 11:11-12, 15? Certainly it is. Is it used absolutely (meaning all Gentiles without exception) or is it used relatively (meaning all Gentiles without distinction)? Relative, otherwise Christ's teaching on hell would be erroneous. But if *kosmos* refers to Gentiles in a relative sense in Romans 11 (and it does), is this how the apostle John uses it in I John 2:2? I believe it is. But can it be established whether John, who was probably writing from Ephesus in Asia Minor, was writing first of all to Jewish believers in his epistle while living in a Gentile environment? Arthur Pink cites four convincing reasons that he was. They are:

> (1) In the opening verse he says of Christ, "Which we have seen with *our* eyes ... and *our* hands have handled." How impossible it would have been for the apostle Paul to have commenced any of *his* epistles to *Gentile* saints with such language! (2) "Brethren, I write no new commandment unto you, but an old commandment which *ye* had *from the beginning"* (I John 2:7). The "beginning" here referred to is the beginning of the public manifestation of Christ—in proof compare 1:1, 2:13, etc. Now these believers, the apostle tells us, *had* the *"old* commandment" *from the beginning.* This was true of *Jewish* believers, but it was not true of *Gentile* believers. (3) "I write unto you, fathers, because *ye have known* Him from the beginning" (2:13). Here, again, it is evident that it is *Jewish* believers that are in view. (4) "Little children, it is the last time: and as *ye have heard* that Antichrist shall come, even now are there many antichrists; whereby we know that it is the last time. *They* went out from *us,* but they were not of us" (2:18, 19). These brethren to whom John wrote *had* "heard" from Christ Himself that Antichrist should come (see Matt. 24). The "many antichrists" whom John declares "went out *from us"* were all *Jews,* for during the first century none but *a Jew* posed as the Messiah. Therefore, when John says "He is the propitiation for *our* sins," he can only mean for the sins of *Jewish believers.* (It is true that many things in John's Epistle apply equally

to believing Jews and believing Gentiles. Christ is the Advocate of
the one, as much as of the other.)[25]

Furthermore, when John added, "and not for ours only, but
also for the sins of the whole world," he signified that—

Christ was the propitiation for the sins of the *Gentile believers too,*
for, ... 'the world' is a term *contrasted* from Israel. This
interpretation is unequivocally established by a careful comparison
of I John 2:2 with John 11:51, 52, which is a strictly parallel
passage: 'And this spake he not of himself: but being high priest
that year, he prophesied that Jesus should die for that nation; And
not for that nation only, but that also He should gather together in
one the children of God that were scattered abroad.' Here Caiaphas,
under inspiration, made known *for whom* Jesus should 'die.' Notice
now the correspondency of his prophecy with this declaration of
John's: 'He is the propitiation for our (believing Israelites) sins.'
'He prophesied that Jesus should die for that nation.' 'And not for
ours only.' 'And not for that nation only.' 'But also for the whole
world'—that is, Gentile believers scattered throughout the earth.
'He should gather together in one the children of God that were
scattered abroad.'[26]

Conclusion

The reader will have to judge for himself which of the four
universalistic interpretations of I John 2:2 is the most biblical. It
seems to me that the ethnological view best interprets the
meaning of the immediate and general context. It is my position
along with most historic Calvinists that in the first part of I John
2:2—

the believing *Jews* alone are intended, of whom John was one; and
the addition [last part of the verse] is not an extending of the
propitiation of Christ to *others than believers,* but only to *other
believers* [i.e., Gentile believers]. If it might be granted that in the

---

[25]Arthur W. Pink, *The Atonement* (Venice, Florida: Chapel Library, n.d.),
13-14.

[26]*Ibid.,* 14.

first branch [first part of the verse] all believers then living were comprehended, who might presently be made partakers of this truth [geographical view], yet the increase or accession [last part of the verse] must be, by analogy, only those who *were to be* in after ages [eschatological view] and remoter places than the name of Christ had then reached unto,—even all those who, according to the prayer of our Savior, John xvii. 20, should believe on his name to the end of the world.[27]

It can be readily seen from this interpretation that the geographical and eschatological views are both included within the ethnological interpretation. The geographical view is included by its very nature; that is, that God's elect are scattered among the Jews and Gentiles throughout the whole world. And it should be apparent that the ethnological and eschatological views are closely related as seen in John 3:16, 17, where both are consecutively set forth. But Warfield's eschatological view, by itself, tends to minimize the geographical or world-wide aspect of Christ's atonement and fails to mention the ethnological view. Although all three views are in harmony with the scriptural doctrine of election, it is concluded that the geographical and eschatological views do not, by themselves, fully answer the intention of the apostle John in I John 2:2. Rather it seems that John wants to make it clear to his readers in this verse (as well as John 3:16) that the Old Testament particularism in relation to the nation of Israel is now past, so he uses the universal term "whole world." Christ has now brought in the New Covenant and has prepared the way for New Testament universalism—a divine universalism which teaches that Messiah is the saviour of the spiritual seed of Abraham, who testify in due season[28] that they

---

[27]Owen, *The Death of Death in the Death of Christ*, 226.

[28]"The 'due season' comprises the entire *new* dispensation. ... Not during the old dispensation but only during the new can the mystery be fully revealed that *all men,* Gentiles as well as Jews, are now on an equal footing; that is, that the Gentiles have become 'fellow-heirs and fellowmembers of the body and fellow-partakers of the promise in Christ Jesus through the gospel' (Eph. 3:6;

are none other than Christ's ransomed ones, God's elect. It is for this very reason that the sovereign grace ambassador of Christ knows that God will make "known the riches of his glory on the vessels of mercy" by calling them out "not of the Jews only, but also of the Gentiles" (Rom. 9:23-24). Therefore, he carries out the great commission with full assurance and much boldness, enduring "all things for the elect's sake, that they may also obtain the salvation which is in Christ Jesus with eternal glory" (II Tim. 2:10)

---

cf. Eph. 2:11, 12)." Cf. William Hendriksen, *New Testament Commentary: Exposition of the Pastoral Epistles* (Grand Rapids: Baker Book House, 1957), 99.

FOUR INTERPRETATIONS OF I JOHN 2:2

"And he (Christ) is the propitiation (*hilasmos*) for our sins; and not for ours only, but also for the sins of the whole (*holou*) world (*kosmou*)"

Interpretation	The Extent of Propitiation (*hilasmos*) in I John 2:2	Meaning of "our sins" in I John 2:2	Extent of Propitiation (*hilasmos*) in Other NT Salvation Passages	Meaning of "the whole (*holos*) world (*kosmos*)" in I John 2:2	Extent of "world" (*kosmos*) in Other NT Salvation Passages
[1]*Generical* (Universal—All Mankind—the World of Mankind)	Christ appeased God's wrath & secured the *possibility* of salvation for all mankind without exception. Propitiation becomes *actual* for the elect by the act of faith	Believers' sins throughout history—the elect	The extent in Rom. 3:25, Heb. 2:17 and I John 4:10 is not considered	Includes the sins of all mankind throughout history—both the elect and the non-elect	"World" is assumed to mean everybody without exception, both elect and non-elect
[2]*Geographical* (World-wide)	Christ appeased God's wrath & secured the salvation of the elect only	Believers in Asia Minor at the time I John was written	Restricted to believers, i.e., God's elect	Includes the world of believers outside Asia Minor	Ultimately restricted to God's elect; it never includes the non-elect in a salvation context
[3]*Eschatological* (Future Saved World)	Christ appeased God's wrath & secured the salvation of the elect only	The present believing world	Restricted to believers, i.e., God's elect	Refers to the future believing world; see John 1:29	Ultimately restricted to God's elect; it never includes the non-elect in a salvation context
[4]*Ethnological* (Jew and Gentile World)	Christ appeased God's wrath & secured the salvation of the elect only—both Jew & Gentile	Jewish believers, especially in Asia Minor; see I John 1:1; 2:13, 18-19	Restricted to believers, i.e., God's elect, whether Jew or Gentile; see Rom. 3:25; Heb. 2:17; I John 4:10	Refers to believers, especially those outside Asia Minor; see John 11:51-52	Ultimately restricted to God's elect, especially Gentile believers (see John 3:16; Acts 11:18); it never includes the non-elect in a salvation context

[1]Held with variation, by both Arminians and modified Calvinists. " ... Christ is the *actual* propitiation for believers' sins through faith, and the *potential* propitiation only for the sins of the non-elect.

[2]Held by some Historic Calvinists. " ... Christ is the propitiation for the sins of believers *both in and outside Asia Minor*."

[3]Held by some Historic Calvinists. " ... Christ is the propitiation for the sins of both the elect in the present world and in the *future world* where all the sins of that world will be taken away."

[4]Held by some Historic Calvinists. " ... Christ is the propitiation for the sins of *both Jewish and Gentile believers* [Ethnological World] regardless of place [Geographical World] or time [Eschatological World]."

APPENDIX III

RECONCILIATION IN II CORINTHIANS 5:19 (A DOCTRINAL STUDY ON THE EXTENT OF THE ATONEMENT)

Introduction

In discussing the design or extent of the atonement, there are three key doctrinal terms which are related to the priestly sacrifice of Christ on earth, that is, to the finished work of Christ. These terms are redemption, propitiation and reconciliation. Evangelical Arminians and Calvinistic "four point" universalists or modified Calvinists[1] hold that there is a universal design of the atonement which provides salvation for all mankind without exception or which places all of Adam's posterity in a savable state. They contend that there is a twofold application of these three doctrinal terms—an actual application for those who believe, a provisional application for those who die in unbelief. The historic "five point" or consistent Calvinist[2] asserts that these terms have no substitutionary reference with respect to the non-elect. In contrast to the former who hold to an indefinite atonement, the consistent Calvinist, who holds to a definite atonement, sees no purpose, benefit or comfort in a redemption that does not redeem, a propitiation that does not propitiate or a reconciliation that does not reconcile, which would be the case if these terms were applicable to the non-elect.

For those who have wrestled with the extent of the atonement, they are acutely aware that there are three problem verses[3] which the five point Calvinist must scripturally answer if he is to consistently sustain a biblical position before the modified Calvinist that the saving design of the atonement is intended by

---

[1] For a description of Evangelical Arminians and Calvinistic "four point" universalists or modified Calvinists see footnote 1 to Appendix I above.

[2] See footnote 2 to Appendix I above.

[3] See footnote 3 to Appendix II above.

the triune God only for the elect. These verses are II Peter 2:1, which pertains to redemption; I John 2:2, which pertains to propitiation; and II Corinthians 5:19, which pertains to reconciliation. If the particular redemptionist can scripturally establish in any of these verses that God's design of the atonement does not extend to the non-elect, then the theological case for the unlimited redemptionist crumples. In summary, if universal reconciliation in II Corinthians 5:19 cannot be biblically established, then what purpose does a universal redemption in II Peter 2:1 or a universal propitiation in I John 2:2 serve? Can it be true that God reconciled the non-elect, for whom His wrath will never be propitiated (satisfied or appeased) by virtue of Christ's death or that He has been reconciled by virtue of Christ's death to the non-elect upon whom His condemning wrath eternally abides (John 3:36)?

The purpose of this doctrinal appendix is to approach theologically II Corinthians 5:19, which relates to reconciliation—the last of the three major doctrinal terms. May those who have believed through grace find this appendix of much help in their doctrinal study of the Word of God.

A Distinction in Terminology

Before discussing the extent of reconciliation in II Corinthians 5:19, it is necessary to state the meaning of the two theological terms used in connection with the New Testament doctrine of reconciliation. The two terms are "soteric reconciliation," which refers to the saving aspect of reconciling the rational creation (fallen mankind), and "cosmic reconciliation,"[4] which refers to the world-wide aspect of reconciling the non-rational creation.

---

[4]The terms "soteric" and "cosmic" reconciliation are not original with me but were taken from an article by John Murray. Cf. his article entitled: "The Reconciliation," *Westminster Theological Journal,* XXIX (November 66-May 67), 1-23.

Soteric Reconciliation

The term "soteric reconciliation" is used to distinguish it from the cosmic aspect of reconciliation, which is set forth in Colossians 1:16, 20. Soteric or saving reconciliation has special reference to reconciling mankind in their lost estate (cf. Roman. 5:8-11; Eph. 2:13-18; II Cor. 5:18-20; Col. 1:21-23), not with reconciliation in its cosmic or world-wide non-rational creation aspect, which includes the compulsive submission of all enemies of Christ and the removal of the curse upon the whole creation (cf. Col. 1:20; Rom. 8:18-23; I Cor. 15:24-25). Therefore, soteric reconciliation may be theologically defined as—

> a twofold change in the relationship between God and man as wrought objectively through the death of Christ, which results in God's relationship toward His people being changed from enmity to love and blessing, and as wrought subjectively in His people by divine bestowal, which results in man's relationship toward God being changed from enmity to love when the word of reconciliation is genuinely received as evidenced by repentance toward God and faith toward the Lord Jesus Christ.

The end result of Christ's accomplished and applied soteric reconciliation is that peace is made between both God and man. As soteric reconciliation has to do with the positive aspect of God's relationship to man, namely, in the death of Christ making peace between God and man, so propitiation has to do with the negative aspect of God's relationship to man, namely, in the death of Christ satisfying God's just wrath against man's sins.

The results of the soteric reconciliation wrought by Christ are twofold. First, God was reconciled "by the death of his Son" (Rom. 5:10) so that He might save from wrath those who are objectively and actually reconciled in this death, namely, His elect. Second, the elect are being subjectively and experientially reconciled to God in due season as the Spirit of God imparts to them the gift of repentance and faith through the miracle of the new birth.

Although the above definition for soteric reconciliation states that both God and man are reconciled, the matter of determining who was reconciled, God or man, or both, does not have to be settled to prove the extent of soteric reconciliation. It should be remembered, however, that the position that man only is reconciled was never taught or believed in orthodox church history before it was infiltrated by the folly of sixteenth century Socinianism.[5]

II Corinthians 5:19

Modern day Calvinistic universalists say that there is only a manward aspect in soteric reconciliation. Their key proof text is II Corinthians 5:19. One writer states that "in verse 19 it is declared that the world (*kosmos,* which term is never by any stretch of exegesis made to represent the elect who are saved out of it) is reconciled to God."[6] "World" is thus understood in a soteric sense in this verse by the modified Calvinist but in a generic or universal sense, which includes all mankind without exception. Therefore universal reconciliation for all mankind in an absolute sense is claimed. Concerning universal soteric reconciliation in II Corinthians 5:19, it is stated by the four point Calvinist that "the world is so altered in its position respecting the holy judgments of God through the cross of Christ that God is

---

[5]Socinianism is "a deviation from orthodoxy within Protestantism named after Fausto Sozzini (or Socinus, 1539-1604), a product of the radical skepticism of the Italian Renaissance. He denied the full deity of Christ, predestination, original sin, total inability, atonement by penal substitution and justification by faith; the 'salvation' he retained was gained by works. ... With the advent of deism in the eighteenth century, Socinian thought became predominant in many circles, both General Baptists and English Presbyterians being widely contaminated. In 1774 the first Unitarian (= Socinian) church as such was formed in London." O. Raymond Johnston, "Socinianism," *Baker's Dictionary of Theology*, ed. by Everett F. Harrison and others (Grand Rapids: Baker Book House, 1960), 490.

[6]Lewis Sperry Chafer, *Systematic Theology* (Dallas, Texas: Dallas Seminary Press, 1948), 3:91.

not now imputing their sin unto them. The world is thus rendered savable."[7]

The Issue

Therefore, the issue between modified and consistent Calvinists concerning reconciliation in II Corinthians 5:19 is not whether reconciliation is to be understood soterically or cosmically, but the question is: "What is the extent of 'world' with reference to soteric reconciliation?" Does it have reference to all mankind without exception, or to all mankind without distinction (i.e., some "out of every kindred and tongue, and people, and nation" who are ultimately manifested as God's elect)? Is soteric reconciliation absolute[8] or relative in extent? Does it include all mankind absolutely without exception (i.e., generically or universally) or does it refer to some of all mankind relatively without distinction? The modified Calvinist says that the reconciliation of Christ in II Corinthians 5:18, 19 has provisionally reconciled the "world" (meaning all mankind without exception). By this it is meant that God has rendered all mankind *savable* upon *condition* that they believe.

The meaning of the term "world"

Is explained in the next phrase.—The meaning of the term "world" in II Corinthians 5:19 is revealed in the phrase which immediately follows, namely, that God was in Christ "not imputing their [the world's] trespasses unto them." The point should be obvious. The phrase "not imputing their trespasses unto them" definitely means that the "world" (whoever they are) has not its (their) sins imputed to them. But it is evident from

---

[7]*Ibid.*, 7:262.

[8]I believe that the theological problem on the extent of reconciliation in II Corinthians 5:19 would vanish if the representative principle were understood or remembered by those who want to make *kosmos* absolute and thereby that reconciliation is generically universal, in a provisional sense, for all mankind.

Scripture that many of mankind do have their sins imputed to them; otherwise none would or could be condemned by God for his sins. Then, does this not require that "world" must be interpreted restrictively in this verse? Does not the context speak of an effectual reconciliation for "them" who have not their sins imputed? Are not the "them" of verse 19 the same ones for whom Christ was made sin, the same ones who become "the righteousness of God in him" in verse 21? Therefore, does not "world" in verse 19 speak of those upon whom soteric or saving reconciliation is being bestowed in due season; that is, those who are and who will be a new creation in Christ (cf. v. 17)? Is not this in harmony with the words of the Lord who says in John 17:20: "Neither pray I for these alone, but for them also which shall believe on me through their word"?

Does not mean all mankind without exception.—In reply to those who say that "world" refers to all mankind distributively, Owen writes that God's reconciling action in Christ holds out an—

> effectual work of reconciliation. Now, this must be either an absolute reconciliation or a conditionate. If *absolute,* why are not all actually and absolutely reconciled, pardoned, justified? If conditionate, then,—First, How can a *conditionate reconciliation* be reconciled with that which is actual? Secondly, Why is no condition here mentioned? Thirdly, What is that condition? Is it faith and believing? Then the sense of the words must be either,—first, "God was in Christ, reconciling a believing world unto himself," of which there is no need, for believers are reconciled; or, secondly, "God was in Christ reconciling an unbelieving world unto himself, upon condition that it do believe"; that is, upon condition that it be not unbelieving; that is, that it be reconciled. Is this the mind of the Holy Spirit? Fourthly, If this reconciliation of the world consists (as it doth) in a non-imputation of sin, then this is either of all their sins, or only of some sins. If of some only, then Christ saves only from some sins. If of all, then of unbelief also, or it is no sin; then all the men in the world must needs be saved, as whose unbelief is pardoned. The *world* here, then, is only the world of blessed,

pardoned believers, who [become] "the righteousness of God in Christ."[9]

Is supported by biblical theology.—Romans 5:9-10 lends strong support to the five point Calvinist position on the extent of soteric reconciliation. The teaching of Paul in this passage is that those for whom Christ died are now being "justified by his blood" and "shall be saved from wrath." Paul logically proceeds and states that these are the same ones who "were reconciled to God by the death of his Son ... [and] shall be saved by his [resurrection] life" (cf. Rom. 6:5). This affirms what I believe to be the strongest biblical proof for definite atonement, namely, that the death of Christ is the basis and surety for the Father's giving "all things" in Romans 8:32 to those for whom Christ died. Among some of the gifts of saving grace in the context of the "all things" are effectual calling, justification and glorification. Now, anyone effectually called, justified and glorified must be saved, and this can refer only to those who truly believe, God's elect.

Is not supported by a generical interpretation of John 3:16.—In anticipation of a commonly stated defense for universal reconciliation, it should be observed that those who say that "world" in II Corinthians 5:19 refers to all mankind without exception usually do so upon their understanding of the love of God for the world from such passages as John 3:16. However, the following quote from Warfield's excellent sermon on John 3:16, in my judgment, defrocks this interpretation of "world" in both John 3:16 and II Corinthians 5:19. For, if those who hold to a universal soteric reconciliation in a generic sense—

> persist in reading the text [John 3:16] thus [absolutely, make] "the world" mean each and every man that lives on the earth, ... what ...

---

[9]John Owen, *The Death of Death in the Death of Christ* (reprinted from Vol. 10 of Owen's Works, published in 1852 by Johnstone and Hunter, Edinburgh, and ed. by William H. Goold; London: The Banner of Truth Trust, 1959), 227-28.

does it declare that the love of God has done for them? Just open a way of salvation before men, give them an opportunity to save themselves. ... Is this, then, the measure of the immeasurable love of God—that He barely opens a pathway to salvation before sinful men, and stops right there; does nothing further for them—leaving it to their own unassisted initiation whether they will walk in it or not? Surely this cannot be the teaching of the text.[10]

Conclusion

If the doctrinal appendixes on redemption in II Peter 2:1 and propitiation in I John 2:2 (Appendixes I and II, respectively) have established that redemption and propitiation are to be restricted to those who believe, God's elect, then what purpose would a universal reconciliation serve for the non-elect? Would God reconcile those whom He did not redeem? Has God been propitiated (satisfied) for the sins of those whom He will pour out His eternal wrath in the lake of fire? Certainly not! It is concluded, therefore, that II Corinthians 5:19 does not teach that all men distributively (i.e., without exception) have been reconciled either provisionally or hypothetically. Rather it teaches that God is and has been reconciling His people (without distinction from the world in a relative sense) one by one[11]

---

[10]Benjamin Breckinridge Warfield, *Biblical and Theological Studies,* ed. Samuel G. Craig (Nutley, N.J.; The Presbyterian and Reformed Publishing Co., 19752), 507-508.

[11]The verb "was" (*ēn*) is in the imperfect tense and is grammatically linked with "reconciling" (*katallassōn*), which is in the present tense. The present tense of "reconciling" is better understood to add an iterative idea (some say a customary or gnomic idea) to the progressive stress of the periphrastic imperfect ("was ... reconciling"), which is grammatically permissible and historically true in the application of reconciliation. Some attempt to take "was" with "in Christ" (*en Christō*) rather than with "reconciling" to stress the deity of Christ (i.e., God was in Christ). But the context shows that "God" (*Theos*) refers to the Father and not to Christ's deity, although certainly Christ is deity. Furthermore, it is without parallel in Paul's and the other New Testament writings to say that "was" goes with "in Christ" as a way of affirming the deity of Christ. The "in Christ" is a dative of sphere and is in

throughout history and will continue doing so until the last one of His sheep is added to His fold. Then, and then only, will the shepherd of the sheep return, but not before, for "the Lord is not slack concerning his promise, as some men count slackness; but is longsuffering to us-ward, not willing[12] that any should perish, but that all should come to repentance" (II Pet. 3:9).

---

harmony with the theological truth of representative headship as is the whole context, especially verses 14-15 and 21. Cf. Murray, "Reconciliation," 15.

[12]Although I believe in the free *proclamation* of the gospel, I have become concerned with the manner in which present day five point Calvinists are using dubious language, especially with reference to a conditional and unconditional will of God, to establish a warrant for the "free offer" of the gospel to all mankind universally. It is possible that pursuing this distinction will lead men to believe that they can repent at any time because Christ died for them. It may, in time, water-down historic Calvinism and lead to error just as surely as the false distinction between natural ability and moral inability led to error in 17th century French Calvinism and 18th and 19th century New England Calvinism. Hence, I disagree with those five point Calvinists (including John Calvin, the Marrow Men of early 18th century Scotland and some contemporary Calvinists) who understand "willing" (*boulomenos*) in II Peter 3:9 to refer to the revealed will or desire of God that may not come to pass and different from His secret or decretive will that will come to pass. They use this approach to help justify the "free offer" of the gospel to all mankind without exception. Although I believe in preaching a universal gospel to all mankind without exception (because all in their lost state are outside the covenant fold of God), I do not believe II Peter 3:9 teaches that God desires the repentance and salvation of all mankind without exception. The word used in this verse is *boulomai,* which often, in context, as here, refers to the decretive will of God; that is, His will stemming from the eternal purpose of the Godhead. Neither do I believe that God's will as desire (*thelō*), which logically proceeds from inclination, supports His desire to save all mankind without exception, for what God's soul "desireth (*thelō*), even that he doeth" (Job 23:13). In summary, I believe that God's will, both as desire and decree, will come to pass and that one of the contextual means to understanding such passages as Ezekiel 18:23,22 and 33:11 is that God, *humanly speaking, does not delight or take pleasure* in willing "the death of the wicked" in and of itself. The context in Ezekiel 18 and 33 is stressing the *physical* death of God's disobedient covenant people, Israel. But God does desire and ordain the condemnation of certain ones of old, does He not (Jude 4)? But why? I answer, to "make his

power known" and magnify His justice while enduring "with much longsuffering the vessels of wrath fitted to destruction" (Rom. 9:22). "Even so, Father: for so it seemed good in thy sight" (Matt. 11:26). Therefore, I understand the "us-ward," "any" and "all" of II Peter 3:9 to refer to the "beloved" of verses 1 and 8, God's elect, who come to repentance one by one as God effectually calls them in time, "not of the Jews only, but also of the Gentiles" (Rom. 9:24). See William Hendriksen, *A Commentary on the Gospel of John* (two vols. in one; London: The Banner of Truth Trust, 1959), 2:366.

APPENDIX IV

AN ANNOTATED DOCTRINAL SERMON OUTLINE ON DEFINITE ATONEMENT[1]

The Design of the Atonement or for Whom Did Christ Die as a Substitute?

"For God so loved the world, that he gave his only begotten Son, that whosoever believeth in him should not perish, but have everlasting life" (John 3:16).

Scripture reading: Romans 8:28-39

Introduction.

A. *Personal conviction.*—Make clear that what is called the five points of Calvinism perfectly harmonizes with the biblical truth that salvation belongs to the triune Jehovah. Therefore, none of the doctrinal points can be scripturally or logically rejected without rejecting all of them: T-U-L-I-P. NOTE: Read quote from Charles Haddon Spurgeon, *The Early Years,* p. 168.[2]

B. *Purpose of this doctrinal sermon.*—In order to help recover the old, authentic, biblical gospel and to help bring evangelical teaching, preaching, and practice back into line with

---

[1] A sermon preached at the first Annual Weekend Sovereign Grace Fellowship Doctrinal Conference in Salado, Texas, October 4-6, 1974.

[2] "I have my own private opinion that there is no such thing as preaching Christ and Him crucified, unless we preach what nowadays is called Calvinism. It is a nickname to call it Calvinism; Calvinism is the gospel, and nothing else. I do not believe we can preach the gospel, if we do not preach justification by faith without works; nor unless we preach the sovereignty of God in His dispensation of grace; nor unless we exalt the electing, unchangeable, eternal, immutable, conquering love of Jehovah; nor do I think we can preach the gospel, unless we base it upon the special and particular redemption of His elect and chosen people which Christ wrought out upon the cross." Charles Haddon Spurgeon, *The Early Years* (the first vol. in a rev. ed. of his autobiography, originally compiled by his wife and private secretary; London: The Banner of Truth Trust, 1967), 168.

it, the purpose of this message is to set forth, in a positive manner, what I believe to be the strongest theological and biblical proof for the third of the five points of Calvinism; the doctrine of Limited atonement—a doctrine better referred to by the terms "definite atonement" or "particular redemption."

Outline

    I.   The Importance of the Doctrine of Definite Atonement.

    II. Proof for the Doctrine of Definite Atonement from the Eternal, Immutable, Distinguishing Love of the Triune God.

    III. Objections to the Doctrine of Definite Atonement.

    IV. Applications of the Doctrine of Definite Atonement.

I. *THE IMPORTANCE OF THE DOCTRINE OF DEFINITE ATONEMENT.* The question at hand is: "What is the scriptural teaching on the design of the atonement, or for whom did Christ die as a substitute?" The answer to this question is important in at least three areas. It is important:

A. *Theologically.*—Four alternatives.

    1. *Pure universalism.*—Christ died to save all men without exception.

    2. *Arminian universalism.*—Christ died to provide salvation for all men without exception but not to save anyone in particular-only those who believe of their own free will.

    3. *Calvinistic universalism.*—Christ died to provide salvation for all mankind without exception, but it is only applied to the elect on the condition of faith (because faith is not included within the purchase of Christ for it is divinely bestowed, according to God's sovereign will at conversion).

      4. *Calvinistic particularism.*—Christ died a substitutionary death only for the elect who are saved through the means of faith.

B. *Historically.*—It is a historical fact that the theological descendants of those who have accepted Arminian or Calvinistic universalism have not stopped with an unlimited atonement or indefinite atonement, but they have gone on, either in that or subsequent generations, to deny the doctrines of original sin, total depravity, unconditional election, the substitutionary atonement, hell, the authority and inerrancy of Scripture, and, ultimately, the necessity of believing in Christ as the only way of salvation. NOTE: Read quotes from A. A. Hodge, *The Atonement*, p. 238[3] and Emmons[4]—an example from New England Theology.

---

[3]"Unquestionably there is no compromise between Arminianism and Calvinism. Those who attempt to stand between must content themselves with treading the air while they receive the fire of both sides. We do not object to Calvinistic Universalism ... because of any danger with which—when considered as a final position—threatens orthodoxy. We distrust it rather because it is not a final position, but is the first step in the easy descent of error." Archibald Alexander Hodge, *The Atonement* (reprint of 1867 ed.; Cherry Hill, New Jersey: Mack Publishing Company, n.d.), 238.

[4]A little over one century ago one of the most influential men in New England theology, Nathaniel Emmons (a theological adherent of Samuel Hopkins), boldly asserted: "I know that some Calvinists maintain that the first sin of Adam is imputed to his posterity; that the righteousness of Christ is imputed to believers for their justification; that sinners are under natural inability to turn from sin to holiness; and that Christ made atonement for the elect only. I grant these are gross absurdities, or mere wens and protuberances, which must be pared off from true Calvinism, in order to make it appear consistent with both reason and Scripture. Accordingly, modern Calvinists readily surrender their formerly untenable outposts and now find it easier to defend their citadel against all attacks of their most numerous adversaries [especially the Unitarians]." Edwards Amasa Park, *Memoir of Nathaniel Emmons* (Boston: Congregational Board of Publication, 1861), 430.

C. *Personally.*—Departure from the doctrine of definite atonement has affected the message and methods of evangelism. It has:

    1. *Affected the message of evangelism.*—God's grace and the cross work of Christ have been belittled because of a man-centered theology in evangelism. As a result, man thinks he can turn the grace of God on or off at will ("Tap Water Theology"). Many universal redemptionists teach that Christ's death was a single provision for sin which has a twofold application:[5]

      a. *For the non-elect*—a legal provision only, so that God may justly condemn them for the sin of unbelief.

      b. *For the elect*—a legal and moral provision, so that God may justly save, rather than condemn them.

    2. *Affected the methods of evangelism.*—Ultimately, preaching an indefinite atonement leads one to believe that Christ saves man with man's help. NOTE: Read quote from J. I. Packer, Introductory Essay to John Owen's *The Death of Death in the Death of Christ*, p. 14.[6]

---

[5]Cf. Norman F. Douty, *The Death of Christ* (Swengel, Pennsylvania: Reiner Publications, 1972), 47-50.

[6]"When we come to preach the gospel, our false preconceptions make us say just the opposite of what we intend. We want (rightly) to proclaim Christ as Saviour; yet we end up saying that Christ, having made salvation possible, has left us to become our own saviours. It comes about in this way. We want to magnify the saving grace of God and the saving power of Christ. So we declare that God's redeeming love extends to every man and that Christ has died to save every man, and we proclaim that the glory of divine mercy is to be measured by these facts. And then, in order to avoid universalism, we have to depreciate all that we were previously extolling and to explain that, after all, nothing that God and Christ have done can save us unless we add something to it; the decisive factor which actually saves us is our own believing. What we say comes to this—that Christ saves us with our help; and what that means,

II. *PROOF FOR THE DOCTRINE OF DEFINITE ATONEMENT FROM THE ETERNAL, IMMUTABLE, DISTINGUISHING LOVE OF THE TRIUNE GOD.*

A. *God's love.*—If I were asked, "What is the strongest theological support for definite atonement?" I would unhesitatingly answer, "The eternality and immutability of God's special distinguishing love." If I were asked, "What is the strongest biblical support for definite atonement?" I would unhesitatingly answer, "Romans 8:32 and John 3:16 in context, in that order."

1. *Defined.*—Two aspects—the goodness of God in general and the goodness of God in particular.[7]

a. *The goodness of God in general*—"that perfection of God which He deals kindly with all His creatures." (Cf. Luke 6:35; Matt. 5:45)

b. *The goodness of God in particular*—"that perfection in which God delights in the contemplation of His own infinite perfections as it is extended and reflected in those rational creatures whom He has loved with an everlasting love."

2. *The moving cause of redemption.*—John 3:16; I John 3:1; 3:16; 4:9, 10.

3. *Immutable.*—James 1:17.

4. *Eternal.*—Jer.31:3.

5. *Distinguishing.*

---

when one thinks it out, is this—that we save ourselves with Christ's help. This is a hollow anticlimax." J. I. Packer, Introductory Essay to John Owen's *The Death of Death in the Death of Christ* (added to a reprint from Vol. 10 of Owen's Works, published in 1852 by Johnstone and Hunter, Edinburgh, and ed. by William H. Goold; London: The Banner of Truth Trust, 1959), 14.

[7]Cf. Louis Berkhof, *Systematic Theology* (1st British ed.: London: The Banner of Truth Trust, 1958), 70-71.

a. His distinguishing love is not manifested toward all mankind without exception. (Rom. 9:13; John 17:9)

b. His distinguishing love is self-sacrificial. (John 15:13; Rom. 5:6, 10)

c. Romans 8:32 and John 3:16 in context—the strongest theological and biblical proof for definite atonement in the Bible.

(1). Romans 8:32: "He that spared not his own Son, but delivered him up for us all, how shall he not with him also freely give us all things?" Those who teach an indefinite atonement restrict the term "all" in this verse. Why? Because they have to restrict it, because Paul is stressing that those for whom God spared not His own Son are certain to be called, justified and glorified just as certainly as the fact that Christ died a substitutionary atonement on the cross (cf. context). But if the sacrifice of Christ makes calling, justification and glorification certain (and it does), then what does John 3:16 really teach?

(2). John 3:16: "For God so loved the world, that he gave his only begotten Son, that whosoever believeth in him should not perish, but have everlasting life." Unless it is granted that the term "world" in John 3:16 is to be understood relatively, as referring to both Jews and Gentiles (especially to Gentiles) scattered throughout the geographical world who are ultimately manifested as God's elect through faith and not each and every individual of mankind, then one of the following statements must be granted by those who hold to an indefinite atonement. Either John 3:16 teaches:

(a). That God will save all mankind without exception—universalism, or

(b). That God's redeeming love is distinguishing and particular, both in design and application; otherwise, His love toward the non-elect is temporal and mutable (not eternal and immutable), or He still loves those in hell, or He does not give all things to them to whom He gives His Son.

B. *Summary.*—What is the strongest theological and biblical support for definite atonement? Upon the authority of God's Word, the answer is, "the eternality and immutability of God's special distinguishing love." Based upon Romans 8:32 and John 3:16, therefore, it is asserted that the Bible teaches that Christ died a substitutionary death for sinners. Now, the crux of the question on the extent of the atonement is: "Either Christ died as a substitute, a satisfaction, for the guilt and penalty of the sins of all mankind without exception or He did not." The proof is manifested in the end result of redemption. Only the elect are saved. The atonement, therefore, must be definite not indefinite.

III. ***OBJECTIONS TO THE DOCTRINE OF DEFINITE ATONEMENT.*** **NOTE:** Refer the hearers to Loraine Boettner's work, *The Reformed Doctrine of Predestination*, pp. 282-96.[8]

A. *Practical.*

1. *Objection.*—According to those who believe in an indefinite atonement, the greatest objection to definite

---

[8]Loraine Boettner, *The Reformed Doctrine of Predestination* (Philadelphia: The Presbyterian and Reformed Publishing Company, 1973).

atonement is: "Unless Christ died for all men, the message of God's love and Christ's death must be given with tongue in cheek and with some reservation."[9]

2. *Answer.*—It is not true:

    a. *Historically.*—NOTE: Read quote from Charles Haddon Spurgeon, The New Park Street Pulpit, IV: 135-36.[10]

---

[9]Robert P. Lightner, *The Death Christ Died—A Case for Unlimited Atonement* (Des Plaines, Illinois: Regular Baptist Press, 1967), 15.

[10]"Now, beloved, when you hear any one laughing or jeering at a limited atonement, you may tell him this: General atonement is like a great wide bridge with only half an arch; it does not go across the stream: it only professes to go half way; it does not secure the salvation of anybody. Now, I had rather put my foot upon a bridge as narrow as Hungerford, which went all the way across, than on a bridge that was as wide as the world, if it did not go all the way across the stream. I am told it is my duty to say that all men have been redeemed, and I am told that there is a Scriptural warrant for it—'Who gave himself a ransom for all, to be testified in due time.' Now, that looks like a very, very great argument indeed on the other side of the question. For instance, look here. 'The whole world is gone after him.' Did all the world go after Christ? 'Then went all Judea, and were baptized of him in Jordan.' Was all Judea, or all Jerusalem baptized in Jordan? 'Ye are of God, little children,' and 'the whole world lieth in the wicked one.' Does 'the whole world' there mean everybody? If so, how was it, then, that there were some who were 'of God?' The words 'world' and 'all' are used in seven or eight senses in Scripture; and it is very rarely that 'all' means all persons, taken individually. The words are generally used to signify that Christ has redeemed some of all sorts—some Jews, some Gentiles, some rich, some poor, and has not restricted His redemption to either Jew or Gentile. Leaving controversy, however, I will now answer a question. Tell me, then sir, whom did Christ die for? Will you answer me a question or two, and I will tell you whether He died for *you*. Do you want a Saviour? Do you feel that you need a Saviour? Are you this morning conscious of sin? Has the Holy Spirit taught you that you are lost? Then Christ died for you and you will be saved." Charles Haddon Spurgeon, "Particular Redemption," *The New Park Street Pulpit* (reprint of the 1st ed., published by Alabaster, Passmore and Sons in 1859; Grand Rapids: Zondervan Publishing House, 1964), 4:135-36.

b. *Biblically.*—Christ, in the great commission, expressly commands His disciples to go "into all the world and preach the gospel to every creature" (Mark 16:15).

c. *Theologically.*—Explain the everlasting covenant of redemption as it relates to:

(1). *The universal Gospel call.*—All mankind are outside the covenant. The Gospel call goes forth from the covenant and summons sinners into it. Therefore, it must be a universal call. NOTE: Read quote from Hugh Martin, *The Atonement*, p. 8.[11]

(2). *The logical relationship of the order of the divine decrees to the covenant.*—(Explain)

3. *Objection.*—The sin of unbelief cannot be charged to the non-elect unless Christ died for them (John 3:18).

a. *Answer.*—The sin of unbelief is not the only basis for condemnation. What about imputed sin and actual sin? (Explain)

4. *Biblical.*

a. *Objection.*—Passages in the Bible where universal terminology is used, for example: II Peter 2:1; I John 2:2; and, II Corinthians 5:19.

---

[11]Could the gospel call bring sinners into covenant union with Christ, if the call "itself rested on grounds outside the covenant? Whatever is without the covenant, outside its limits—as an indefinite, unlimited atonement is has nothing to do with the gospel call; can impart to it no validity, no strength, no enlargement; can constitute for it no real basis or foundation. An indefinite atonement, therefore, as pleaded for by some in the interests of the freeness of the gospel call, is one of the most self contradictory and self-negating devices that can be imagined." Hugh Martin, *The Atonement* (reprint of 1871 ed.; Cherry Hill, New Jersey: Mack Publishing Company, n.d.), 8.

b. Answer.—NOTE: Refer the hearers to Appendixes I-III on these passages (previously written as three doctrinal tracts).

IV. *APPLICATIONS OF THE DOCTRINE OF DEFINITE ATONEMENT.* **NOTE:** Refer the hearers to Wayne Mack's, *To God Be the Glory.* [12]

A. *It is scriptural.* (Refer to Part II above.)

B. *It glorifies the triune God.* It glorifies:

1. *His wisdom.*—Only definite atonement is in harmony with the purpose of the trinity in seeking and saving the lost (cf. Luke 19:10).

2. *His justice.*—Only definite atonement is in harmony with the penal satisfaction or substitutionary nature of the atonement. God's holy standards are not relaxed.

3. *His love.*—Only definite atonement is in harmony with the eternal, immutable and distinguishing love of God. (Cf. Part II above)

C. *It motivates the believer.*

1. *To worship and praise.*—O Lord, why me?

2. *To humility.*—Our salvation is all of grace, not of works. NOTE: Read quote from Charles Haddon Spurgeon, The Early Years, pp. 164-65. [13]

---

[12] Wayne Mack, *To God Be the Glory* (Cherry Hill, New Jersey: Mack Publishing Company, 1973).

[13] In Sermon No. 29 of the 1865 volume of the Metropolitan Tabernacle Pulpit, Spurgeon stated: "I believe that very much of current Arminianism is simply ignorance of gospel doctrine." Similarly, in his autobiography he declared: "When I was coming to Christ, I thought I was doing it all myself, and though I sought the Lord earnestly, I had no idea the Lord was seeking me. I do not think the young convert is at first aware of this. I can recall the very day and hour when first I received those truths in my own soul—when they were, as John Bunyan says, burnt into my heart as with a hot iron; and I

3. *To boldness and assurance.*—A multitude beyond number will be saved from "every kindred, and tongue, and people, and nation" (Rev. 5:9).

4. *To service and obedience.*—Definite atonement gives the only logical and biblical basis for evangelism. God has ordained that He will call the elect into covenant union with Christ through faith which comes "by hearing, and hearing by the word of God" (Rom. 10:17).

Closing statements: May what has been taught be of much help to you who have "believed through grace" (Acts 18:27).

"FOR GOD SO LOVED THE WORLD, THAT HE GAVE HIS ONLY BEGOTTEN SON, THAT WHOSOEVER BELIEVETH IN HIM SHOULD NOT PERISH, BUT HAVE EVERLASTING LIFE."

---

can recollect how I felt that I had grown on a sudden from a babe into a man—that I had made progress in Scriptural knowledge, through having found, once for all, the clue to the truth of God. ... I saw that God was at the bottom of it all, and that He was the Author of my faith, and so the whole doctrine of grace opened up to me, and from that doctrine I have not departed to this day, and I desire to make this my constant confession, 'I ascribe my change wholly to God.'" Charles Haddon Spurgeon, *The Early Years,* 164-165.

APPENDIX V: A SUMMARY OF FOUR MAJOR PROBLEM VERSES ON THE EXTENT OF THE ATONEMENT CONCERNING THE WILL OF GOD

PROBLEM VERSE	WHOSE WILL	PROBLEM	UNIVERSAL TERM	ARMINIAN INTERPRETATION	TRANSLATION OF TERM	CALVINIST ANSWER
Matt. 23:27	The Son's	The Son is not able to save if man will not believe	"Jerusalem"	Man can resist Christ's will to save him; "Jerusalem" is extended to include all mankind	"would," *thelō*	Context; Christ speaking in His human nature. See Luke 22:42
Matt. 18:14	The Father's	God wills to save everyone	"one of these little ones"	*God desires to save everyone if they will only believe; "these little ones" are extended to include all mankind	"will," *thelēma*	Context; "these little ones" are believers. See vv. 3-6 & 10-13, especially v. 6
II Pet. 3:9	The Father's	God is not willing that any should perish	"any" & "all"	*God desires to save everyone, but will not overrule man's free will; some perish because they do not will to be saved	"willing," *boulomai*	Context; the "any" & "all" are the "us" ("you") of v. 9 & the "beloved" of vv. 1& 8
I Tim. 2:4	The Father's	God desires all men to be saved but has not decreed to save all men	"all men"	*God desires to save everyone if they will only believe; "all men" is an absolute term, i.e., each and everyone	"will," *thelō*	Context; all classes of men, not all men without exception. See vv. 1-2 & 7. In due time the "ransom" of v. 6 is testified in their salvation

God's will as desire (*thelō* and *thelēma*) does not come to pass in salvation for the *non-elect* because:

- *The Arminian Interpretation:* God desires to save the non-elect, but foresaw that they would not believe and, therefore, did not choose them, although Christ's death is provisional for them.

*- *The Modified Calvinist Interpretation:* God hypothetically desires to save the non-elect, but did not choose them, although Christ's death is provisional for them and serves as a just basis for God to condemn them for their sin of unbelief.

- *The Historic Calvinist Interpretation:* God did not desire to save the non-elect. His will as desire is in perfect harmony with His will in what He does (Job 23:13); universal terms are often used relatively and are always relative in salvation contexts; i.e. all mankind without distinction of class, not all mankind without exception.

God's will as decree (*boulomai, boulē* and *boulēma*) will come to pass in salvation for the elect because:

- *The Arminian Interpretation:* God foresaw who would believe and chose them based upon their foreseen faith in Christ.

*- *The Modified Calvinist Interpretation:* God chose whom He decreed (*boulomai*) would actually believe & be saved because they were dead in sins and could not believe; God has two wills in salvation—a hypothetical will in which He desires (*thelō*) to save the non-elect, but it does not come to pass; a decretive will (*boulomai*) in which He actually purposes to save the elect & it comes to pass. Note that this distinction is used for I Tim. 2:4 where *thelō* is used, but it is not used to explain II Pet. 3:9 where *boulomai* is used.
POINT : A classic inconsistency which receives the fire of both other views!

- *The Historic Calvinistic Interpretation:* God decrees to save the elect for it is they and they alone whom He desires to save; the context where the various terms for "will" are used of God to save the lost always supports this interpretation.

* **POINT:** The Modified Calvinist interpretation is a hopeless compromise between Arminianism and Historic Calvinism.

ANNOTATED SELECTED BIBLIOGRAPHY

Modified Calvinist Works

Armstrong, Brian G. *Calvinism and the Amyraut Heresy.* Madison, Wisconsin: The University of Wisconsin Press, 1969. A scholarly work by a sympathetic Amyraldian which would be better entitled: *"Amyraut and the Calvinism Heresy"* because of the author's theological position.

Chafer, Lewis Sperry. *Systematic Theology.* 8 vols.; Dallas: Dallas Seminary Press, 1948. A standard work for modified Calvinists who are dispensationalists. See volumes 3 and 4 for discussions on the extent of the atonement.

Douty, Norman F. *The Death of Christ.* Swengel, Pennsylvania: Reiner Publications, 1972. A work which will convince some who are wavering on the extent of the atonement; that is, that Christ's substitutionary death was in some sense universal and indefinite in design. However, it may also lead them into the error inherent in the governmental theory of the atonement.

Lightner, Robert P. *The Death Christ Died—A Case for Unlimited Atonement.* Des Plaines, IL: Regular Baptist Press, 1967. A popular work on the subject but weak because of significant exegetical, historical, and logical inconsistencies.

Wardlaw, Ralph. *Discourses on the Nature and Extent of the Atonement.* Glasgow: James Maclehose, 1854. This work and his Systematic Theology—the best theological treatments of the subject from the modified Calvinist position.

_____. *Systematic Theology.* 3 vols.; Edinburgh: Adam and Charles Black, 1857. See vol. 2 for a discussion on the extent of the atonement.

Historic Calvinist Works

Boettner, Loraine. *The Reformed Doctrine of Predestination.* Philadelphia: The Presbyterian and Reformed Publishing Company, 1973. The most thorough and readable work in print on the five points of Calvinism.

Hodge, Archibald Alexander and Martin, Hugh. *The Atonement.* 2 vols. in one; reprint ed.; Cherry Hill, NJ: Mack Publishing Company, n.d. A reprint of two old standard works on the subject. A. A. Hodge's work is second only to John Owen's on the extent of the atonement.

Murray, John. *Redemption Accomplished and Applied.* Grand Rapids: Wm. B. Eerdmans Publishing Company, 1961. Probably the finest brief theological treatment on the doctrine of redemption in print from the historic Calvinist position.

Owen, John. *Works.* 16 vols.; reprint ed.; London: The Banner of Truth Trust, 1965-68. See vol. 10 for the classic treatment on the extent of the atonement from the historic Calvinist viewpoint. The Banner of Truth Trust separately printed a large portion of vol.10 in 1959, but it is no longer in print.

Packer, James I. "Introductory Essay" to John Owen's *The Death of Death in the Death of Christ.* Originally added to a reprint from volume X of Owen's Works published in 1852 by Johnstone and Hunter, Edinburgh, and ed. by William H. Goold; London: The Banner of Truth Trust, 1959. This introduction was first privately printed by Ben K. Howard, M.D., Dallas, Texas, and later by others. A great booklet which strikes at the heart of the theological issue between definite and indefinite atonement.

Palmer, Edwin H. *The Five Points of Calvinism.* Grand Rapids: Baker Book House, 1972. An excellent popular work on the subject.

Reisinger, John G. *Limited Atonement*. Frederick, MD: New Covenant Media, 2002. A succinct, lucid, biblical and fair treatment of the doctrine with practical application.

Steele, David N., and Thomas, Curtis C. *The Five Points of Calvinism*. Philadelphia: Presbyterian and Reformed Publishing Company, 1963 (updated and expanded with S. Lance Quinn in 2004, with a foreword by Roger Nicole.) A lucid treatment of the subject with key scriptural support.

Warfield, Benjamin B. *The Plan of Salvation*. Rev. ed.; Grand Rapids: Wm. B. Eerdmans Publishing Company, 1966. A classic treatment of Calvinistic particularism and how it relates to other theological systems within Christendom.

Other Helpful Works

Adams, James E. *Decisional Regeneration*. Allentown, Pennsylvania: Sword and Trowel Publishers, 1973. Excellent.

Berkhof, Louis. *The History of Christian Doctrines*. British ed.; London: The Banner of Truth Trust, 1969. Probably the best one volume works on the history of Christian doctrine from a Reformed theological viewpoint.

Cunningham, William. *Historical Theology*. 2 vols.; 4th ed.; London: The Banner of Truth Trust, 1960. Excellent.

Hendriksen, William. *A Commentary on the Gospel of John*. Two vols. in one; London: The Banner of Truth Trust, 1954. This work and the following work by a contemporary Reformed scholar—recommended for their fine exegetical treatment of controversial passages on the extent of the atonement.

_____. *New Testament Commentary: Exposition of the Pastoral Epistles.* Grand Rapids: Baker Book House, 1957.

Hodge, Archibald Alexander. *Outlines of Theology.* 1879 rev. ed.; London: The Banner of Truth Trust, 1972. One of the best, if not the best, one volume theologies from the historic Calvinist position.

Horne, Charles M. *Salvation.* Chicago: Moody Press, 1971. An excellent popular book on salvation—well outlined.

Machen, J. Gresham. *What Is Faith?* Grand Rapids: Wm. B. Eerdmans Publishing Company, 1925. The best work on this subject.

Murray, Iain. *The Forgotten Spurgeon.* 2d ed.; London: The Banner of Truth Trust, 1973. Excellent—a work that gives historical validity to A. A. Hodge's classic statement that Calvinistic universalism is not distrusted because of what it teaches as a final position. It is distrusted because it is not a final position, but it is, as Hodge says, "the first step in the easy descent of error."

_____. *The Invitation System.* London: The Banner of Truth Trust, 1967. The best work in print graciously criticizing the modern-day invitational methods from a biblical perspective.

Nicole, Roger. "Amyraldianism." *The Encyclopedia of Christianity,* 1964, 1:184-93. This article and the following one—two fine succinct surveys on the respective subjects by a historic Calvinist.

_____. "The Case for Definite Atonement." *Bulletin of the Evangelical Theological Society,* 10, no. 4 (1967), 199-207.

Pink, Arthur. *The Sovereignty of God.* British rev. ed.; London: The Banner of Truth Trust, 1961. Probably no other book by man in modern times has stimulated evangelical Arminians and modified Calvinists to question their views on God's omnipotence as much as this work. Excellent. The British rev. ed. is an improvement over the original American ed.—some theological inaccuracies were rightly deleted.

Sailer, William S. "The Nature and Extent of the Atonement—A Wesleyan View." *Bulletin of the Evangelical Theological Society,* 10, no. 4 (1967), 189-98. A well written article on behalf of the evangelical Arminian theological position.

Scaer, David. "The Nature and Extent of the Atonement in Lutheran Theology." *Bulletin of the Evangelical Theological Society,* 10, no. 4 (1967), 179-87. A fair presentation from the Lutheran viewpoint, but a view with which, as A. A. Hodge says, the Lutherans must content themselves while they receive the fire from both of the other sides—the evangelical Arminian and historic Calvinist sides.

Shedd, William G. T. *Dogmatic Theology.* 3 vols.; reprint of 1888 ed.; Grand Rapids: Zondervan Publishing House, 1969. A most excellent treatment of God's decrees and attributes is contained in the first volume—an understanding of which is necessary for a sound biblical view on the extent of the atonement.